EATON & LE MAY

Essential Sources of Canadian Law /
Les références essentielles en droit canadien

JOHN EATON

Librarian & Associate Professor,
Faculty of Law, University of Manitoba

DENIS LE MAY

avocat, Barreau du Québec,
Conseiller à la documentation en droit (1975–2006) et Chargé de cours,
Faculté de droit, Université Laval

IRWIN LAW

Eaton & Le May: Essential Sources of Canadian Law / Les références essentielles en droit canadien
© John Eaton and Denis Le May, 2009

Irwin Law
Suite 206
14 Duncan Street
Toronto, Ontario
M5H 3G8

www.irwinlaw.com

ISBN: 1-55221-164-3

Cataloguing in Publication available from Library and Archives Canada

The publisher acknowledges the financial support of the Government of Canada through the Book Publishing Industry Development Program (BPIDP) for its publishing activities.

We acknowledge the assistance of the OMDC Book Fund, an initiative of the Ontario Media Development Corporation.

Printed and bound in Canada.

1 2 3 4 5   13 12 11 10 09

Topics / Matières

Matières / Topics

Acknowledgments

There are a few individuals and entities to thank for their help in the preparation of this book. First of all, acknowledgements are owed to the Legal Research Institute at the University of Manitoba's Faculty of Law, which provided funding to hire two eager law students, Jocelyn Ritchot and Robert Marcoux, to assist in the preliminary amassing of materials related to this project. Thanks and appreciation are extended to Jocelyn and Robert for their enthusiasm and diligence.

Second, I would like to thank my co-author, Denis Le May, whose patience and understanding of my numerous delays and false starts on this project have been limitless. Similarly, Jeffrey Miller, of Irwin Law, is owed a debt of gratitude for his continued willingness to partake in this project despite numerous inaccurate assurances that the book's completion was "just around the corner."

Lastly, I posthumously thank my dear friend, Gordon "Pigfoot" Pearson, whose premature passing in 2007 taught me that life can be unjustly short, and provided inspiration to complete this work in due time. It is to him—and to the memory of our great friendship—that I dedicate this effort.

John Eaton
Winnipeg, Manitoba
January 2009

Introduction

In the years that I have been instructing law students in the process of undertaking legal research, I have always emphasized the importance of beginning one's research with secondary sources. It is in these sources that one finds distillations, explanations, and analyses of the law. In other words, it is in these sources that the researcher finds much of the "heavy-lifting" of legal research and analysis already performed for him. Unless one is particularly expert in an area of law, it is not usually advisable to begin one's research by reading numerous cases and statutes hoping to divine from them the common thread that leads to conclusions as to the state of the law on that issue. As such, it becomes a significant part of the research process to refer to secondary texts and similar materials. This work attempts to inform researchers as to the most "essential" sources on a wide range of legal subtopics that cover almost the entire discipline.

This work grows out of co-author Denis Le May's seminal work on sources of Québec law, *Les références essentielles en droit québécois*, originally published in 1996. It is an attempt to marry an updated version of Le May's sources on Québec law, of which many of the topics are specifically based in the province's *Civil Code*, with sources from the common-law portion of Canada, making this work one which is applicable throughout the entire country — geographically, linguistically, and juridically.

The most challenging part of this work was determining which titles were "essential." No specific definition of "essential" was in my mind throughout this process other than to consider "essential" to be an amalgam of the following attributes: currency, coherence, and comprehensiveness. With this in mind, I spent years personally assessing as many sources as I could and discussing with numerous academics and practitioners their opinions about various titles. This work has grown from that investigation.

Denis and I spent many hours burning up email and telephone lines discussing how best to organize this book. We decided that we would organize each topic alphabetically by its English equivalent and list both English common-law sources with French sources (many of which are grounded in the *Civil Code*). Within each list we would list the titles according to currency, with looseleaf publications listed first (under the presumption that over the years, these will remain the most current) followed by titles in reverse chronological order of publication (i.e., the most recently published are listed first). It should also be noted that it is not always the case that the most essential source is a book. The most cogent work on a topic is sometimes found in a legal encyclopedia, such as the *Canadian Encyclopedic Digest*, or *Halsbury's Laws of*

Canada, or in a specific chapter within a larger textual work. There are even occasions when the most instructive text on an area of law is not even Canadian. The applicability of jurisprudence from throughout the legal "Anglosphere" to Canadian law is sometimes reflected in the significance of other nations' (particularly Britain's) principal texts to Canadian research. As such, there are a few non-Canadian texts included herein.

We have included a short descriptor for each of the topics, orienting the reader as to the nature of the topic and to its jurisdictional fundamentals as it is often important to know which entities are the ultimate creators of the statutes, regulations, and jurisprudence associated with the topic. Each of these topic descriptors is provided in English and in French.

We have attempted, by way of the use of different typefaces, to indicate which information is related to the English, common-law portion of our nation's law and those which are French and relate predominantly to Québec and its blended civil-law/common-law legal system. We hope that this minimizes confusion for the reader.

It is our hope that this work will prove itself useful to a wide range of potential users, including Canadian legal researchers, scholars, librarians, and students. We also see this as a potentially valuable resource to those less familiar with Canadian legal resources and who need assistance in determining where to look for sources on their topic of interest. Self-represented litigants, public libraries, and non-Canadian legal researchers are just a few examples of groups who could put this work to good use. It is our fervent hope that they do and that their research is significantly assisted by reference to this book.

John Eaton
Winnipeg
January 2009

Introduction : Le problème de la doctrine et de ses outils

Dans le jargon juridique, le terme «doctrine» désigne les sources documentaires (monographies et périodiques). Ces dernières sont une des sources du droit, les autres étant la loi et la jurisprudence. La doctrine a toujours été le parent pauvre de la documentation juridique : pauvre par sa rareté, pauvre encore dans son repérage.

Depuis les années 1970, toutefois, la doctrine a connu un essor considérable et jouit maintenant d'une faveur plus grande auprès du monde juridique ; le signalement et le repérage, par contre, souffrent encore de nombreuses lacunes. Cela tient à deux catégories d'explications.

D'une part, le fichier d'une bibliothèque donnée est triplement limité. Premièrement, il ne donne accès qu'aux documents disponibles sur place ; deuxièmement, il ne peut être consulté lui-même qu'en certains endroits (on pense ici aux juristes de l'extérieur des grandes villes, par exemple), et ce, même si on utilise un ordinateur pour interroger un fichier à distance. Troisièmement, l'analyse faite des documents laisse dans l'ombre la couverture d'éléments importants, par exemple le chapitre substantiel d'un traité.

D'autre part, les instruments existants ne répondent pas adéquatement aux besoins du monde juridique pour l'une ou l'autre des raisons suivantes : soit qu'ils ne sont pas tenus à jour (par ex. *Bibliographie de Boult,* arrêtée en 1980) ; soit qu'ils ne couvrent pas les monographies (par ex. *Index to Canadian Legal Periodical Literature*) ou les couvrent de façon incomplète (par ex. *Annuaire de jurisprudence et de doctrine du Québec*) ; soit, encore, qu'ils n'analysent pas en détail les chapitres importants des monographies, quand ils n'ignorent tout simplement pas le Québec.

Les juristes doivent donc consulter plusieurs instruments indépendants les uns des autres pour repérer la documentation pertinente. Dans ce contexte, il n'est pas rare de voir des confrères s'en remettre à leur seule mémoire ou encore aux aléas d'une recherche empirique pour rassembler les linéaments d'une recherche documentaire. Le présent ouvrage désire combler cette lacune et rendre les éléments de départ plus accessibles et prévisibles en présentant *Les références essentielles en droit canadien.* Bien que le sens de ces mots ne fasse aucun doute, nous nous permettons d'expliciter la portée que nous leur avons donnée.

Les références essentielles...

Cette expression couvre tout point de départ ou parcours pour trouver de l'information ; cela comprend d'abord la documentation proprement dite : traités, monographies, thèses, articles de périodiques, bref, ce qu'on appelle normalement la doctrine dans le contexte québécois. Cela comprend ensuite des informations non documentaires liées au droit (listes d'abréviations, banques de données, etc.).

Nous avons rejeté le terme de bibliographie jugé trop limitatif. À l'heure où il est possible d'interroger directement et à distance le fichier d'une grande bibliothèque, il paraissait superflu d'en présenter une simple copie sur papier.

Le titre *Les références essentielles*, en revanche, implique un choix dans plusieurs démarches possibles. Nous n'avons pas voulu recenser tous les titres, nous avons choisi les plus « performants », d'où un certain nombre de conseils disséminés çà et là. Cette idée repose naturellement sur le principe de la sélectivité.

Le nombre de références (titres) par sujet ne dépasse pas dix (10). Normalement il ne s'agit que d'un ordre de grandeur, nullement d'un plafond.

L'hypothèse sous-jacente veut qu'un praticien ou un étudiant disposant de 10 références pertinentes sur l'objet de sa recherche, possède déjà plus qu'un noyau de départ ; il se trouve en fait, en bonne voie d'autonomie.

... en droit canadien

Nous nous adressons tout d'abord à la communauté juridique, de l'étudiant au juge. Rien n'empêche, et nous le souhaitons, que toute personne désirant une suggestion de départ puisse tirer profit du présent ouvrage. On n'a cependant nullement tenu compte des ouvrages de vulgarisation, sauf lorsqu'ils suppléaient à une lacune de la production d'ensemble. De même, on s'en est tenu au droit strictement défini et on n'a pas pris en compte les ouvrages d'autres disciplines portant sur le droit (sociologie, par exemple) ou les ouvrages interdisciplinaires.

Nous couvrons les besoins des juristes canadiens. Ceci implique que tous les domaines fédéraux, provinciaux et municipaux reçoivent une égale attention.

Une première édition de ce livre publiée en français en 1996 chez Wilson et Lafleur offrait une présentation détaillée des ouvrages québécois.

Le présent ouvrage, destiné à l'ensemble des juristes canadiens reflète au mieux les dualités juridiques et linguistiques du Canada. Pour éviter de multiplier les subdivisions sous ces deux aspects et offrir des versions linguistiques ou systématiques en parallèle, les auteurs ont privilégié l'approche suivante :

i) On n'a d'abord délimité le nombre de domaines couverts, autour d'une centaine.

ii) Chaque domaine fait l'objet d'une description en anglais et en français ; selon les cas, les versions peuvent varier en fonction de différences systématiques.

iii) Les sujets sont présentés en ordre alphabétique en anglais ; les intitulés des rubriques en français sont intercalés dans l'ordre alphabétique unique et renvoient à la version anglaise.

iv) Dans chaque rubrique, les ouvrages sont présentés en ordre chronologique, le plus récent en premier, sans égard à la langue.

v) Certains ouvrages sur des matières de compétence provinciale (par ex. le droit des compagnies en Alberta) ont été inclus dans la mesure où ils peuvent être utiles dans l'ensemble du pays à titre supplétif, persuasif ou comparatif.

vi) En ce qui concerne les droits supplétifs proprement dits, les droits français et anglais, on a suivi la règle générale historique et bien fondée au Québec qui renvoie au droit français dans les matières de droit privé et au droit anglais dans les matières de droit public. Ceci dit, plutôt que de mentionner des monographies spécialisées dont on ne pouvait toujours garantir la disponibilité partout au Canada, on a privilégié le renvoi aux grandes encyclopédies, ces dernières comportant le double avantage d'être tenues à jour et de comporter, elles-mêmes, des références bibliographiques. Que ces encyclopédies soient constamment actualisées, nous a dispensés de la mention d'une date d'édition précise ; nous avons suivi la même règle pour les publications à feuilles mobiles.

Autres limites de la couverture

Dans le temps, nous ne donnons que l'édition la plus récente d'un ouvrage. *Quant à la forme,* seul l'écrit est pris en compte ; on n'a nullement mentionné les autres médias (films, vidéos, diapositives, etc.). Toutefois, tous les supports d'écrits disponibles sont inclus : microfilm, bases de données, etc.

Disponibilité des ouvrages

Sauf de rares exceptions, la plupart des ouvrages cités ici sont disponibles dans les grandes bibliothèques juridiques du Québec ainsi que dans les librairies de même type.

Présentation uniforme

Chaque sujet est abordé selon un cadre uniforme. On trouvera tout d'abord un court texte de présentation qui le situe dans le contexte juridico-documentaire et en montre la difficulté, le cas échéant. On trouvera ensuite, en encadré, les références essentielles en ordre d'importance. Dans certains cas, un troisième bloc d'information regroupe des notes complémentaires diverses permettant d'aller plus loin dans la démarche et l'autonomie : on y mentionne des publications en série, des recueils de jurisprudence ou des périodiques, de même que certaines références plus techniques.

Remerciements

Bien que nous prenions la responsabilité de nos choix, nous implorons l'indulgence du lecteur pour toute erreur ou omission. Nous aimerions recevoir commentaires et suggestions en vue d'ajouts et de corrections lors d'une prochaine édition. Cet ouvrage est à jour au 31 octobre 2008.

Denis LeMay

Abbreviations / Abréviations[*]

Abbreviation	Publisher
CBA	Canadian Bar Association
CCH	Commerce Clearing House
CCH Cdn	CCH Canadian
CLB	Canada Law Book
Crswl	Thomson Carswell
CSST	Commission de la santé et de la sécurité au travail du Québec
EM	Emond Montgomery Publications
Irwin	Irwin Law Inc.
LN/B	LexisNexis Butterworths
LSUC	Law Society of Upper Canada
Néopol	Éditions Néopol
OLRC	Ontario Law Reform Commission
OUP	Oxford University Press
S & M	Sweet & Maxwell (U.K.)
SOQUIJ	Société québécoise d'information juridique
Thémis	Éditions Thémis
UBC Press	University of British Columbia Press
U of Cgy	University of Calgary
U of Man	University of Manitoba
U of T Press	University of Toronto Press
W & LaF	Wilson & Lafleur Ltée
Y Blais	Éditions Yvon Blais

* Looseleaf publications are indicated by an (LL) beside the publisher name.

* Les publications à feuilles mobiles sont indiquées par (FM) à côté du nom de la maison d'édition.

I.

ABORIGINAL LAW

Aboriginal law is a complex and multi-dimensional area of the law dealing with Canada's indigenous peoples. It covers as many civil aspects (e.g., who is aboriginal?) as it does territorial ones (land claims, etc.) and at times strays into criminal law (e.g., hunting and fishing offences). Largely a subset of constitutional law, it is a particularly challenging area of practice given its complexity, originality, and dynamism. It is essentially federal in scope (i.e., the *Indian Act*) but is affected by many matters which are provincial in nature. Related topics: CHILDREN AND THE LAW, CONSTITUTIONAL LAW, GAMING & LOTTERIES, HUMAN RIGHTS AND THE *CHARTER OF RIGHTS AND FREEDOMS*.

AUTOCHTONES

Domaine complexe et déroutant, le droit autochtone, en pleine effervescence, couvre autant les aspects civilistes (personnes : qui est autochtone ?) que les dimensions territoriales (les réserves, les revendications). Sous-ensemble congru du droit CONSTITUTIONNEL, le droit AUTOCHTONE, sous le double effet de la *Charte canadienne des droits et libertés et de l'actualité*, touche à un très grand nombre d'aspects. La question autochtone pose au droit des défis inédits par sa complexité, son originalité et son dynamisme.

MACAULAY, MARY LOCKE	*Aboriginal Treaty Rights & Practice*	Crswl (LL)
WOODWARD, JACK	*Native Law*	Crswl (LL)
WILSON, FREDERICA, AND MELANIE MALLET, eds.	*Metis-Crown Relations: Rights, Identity, Jurisdiction, and Governance*	Irwin 2008
OTIS, GHISLAIN	*Droit, territoire et gouvernance des peuples autochtones*	Université Laval 2005
BORROWS, JOHN J., AND LEONARD I. ROTMAN	*Aboriginal Legal Issues: Cases, Materials, and Commentary*, 3d ed.	LN/B 2003
GRAMMOND, SÉBASTIEN	*Aménager la coexistence : les peuples autochtones et le droit canadien*	Y Blais 2003
MAGNET, JOSEPH E., DWIGHT DOREY, AND RUSSEL LAWRENCE BARSH	*Aboriginal Rights Litigation*	LN/B 2003
LAW COMMISSION OF CANADA, AND ASSOCIATION OF IROQUOIS AND ALLIED INDIANS	*In Whom We Trust: A Forum on Fiduciary Relationships*	Irwin 2002
IMAI, SHIN, KATHARINE LOGAN, AND GARY STEIN	*Aboriginal Law Handbook*, 2d ed.	Crswl 1999

* ACCÈS À L'INFORMATION voir PRIVACY LAW & ACCESS TO INFORMATION
* ACCIDENTS DU TRAVAIL ET MALADIES PROFESSIONELLES voir WORKERS' COMPENSATION

2.

ADMINISTRATIVE LAW

An extremely vast field of public law, administrative law is that which deals with numerous federal and provincial boards, tribunals, and commissions and, in its broadest sense, deals with legal aspects of the government in its everyday operation. Much of the interaction of the legal system with the administrative apparatus of government comes in the form of judicial review by the courts of the decisions of boards, tribunals, and commissions. Related topics: AGRICULTURAL & AQUACULTURE LAW, CIVIL PROCEDURE, EDUCATION LAW, ENERGY & NATURAL RESOURCES LAW, ENVIRONMENTAL LAW, IMMIGRATION & CITIZENSHIP, MUNICIPAL LAW, OCCUPATIONAL HEALTH & SAFETY, POLICE & PRIVATE SECURITY LAW, REFUGEES, TAXATION, WORKERS' COMPENSATION.

ADMINSTRATIF (DROIT)

Très vaste domaine du droit public, le droit administratif couvre l'ensemble du gouvernement et de ses émanations (régies et organismes) dans leurs rapports avec les citoyens ainsi que le contrôle judiciaire sur l'administration. Une partie de l'administration décentralisée se trouve étudiée sous MUNICIPAL (DROIT) et SCOLAIRE (DROIT).

COUTU, MICHEL *et al.*	*Droit administratif du travail : tribunaux et organismes spécialisés du domaine du travail*	Y Blais 2007
ROCHETTE, STÉPHANE	*La norme de contrôle judiciaire : synthèse et recueil d'arrêts*	Y Blais 2007
BLAKE, SARA	*Administrative Law in Canada*, 4th ed.	LN/B 2006
GARANT, PATRICE	*Précis de droit des administrations publiques, 4e éd.*	Y Blais 2005
VILLAGGI, JEAN-PIERRE	*L'administration publique québécoise et le processus décisionnel : des pouvoirs au contrôle administratif et judiciaire*	Y Blais 2005
JONES, DAVID PHILLIP, AND ANNE S. DE VILLARS	*Principles of Administrative Law*, 4th ed.	Crswl 2004
MULLAN, DAVID	*Administrative Law: Cases, Texts & Materials*, 5th ed.	EM 2003
MULLAN, DAVID	*Administrative Law*	Irwin 2001
ANISMAN, PHILIP, AND ROBERT F. REID	*Administrative Law: Issues & Practice*	Crswl 1995

3.

ADOPTION

A subset of family law, this area deals specifically with the adoption of minors and is, for the most part, a matter of provincial jurisdiction. Much of adoption law is grounded in the various provincial child protection statutes, but there is relevant federal legislation as well (e.g., the *Divorce Act* and the *Indian Act*). Related topics: CHILDREN AND THE LAW, FAMILY LAW.

ADOPTION

Domaine du droit civil de la famille. L'adoption internationale, également réglementée, fait l'objet de dispositions au livre dixième (droit international privé) du *Code civil du Québec*.

BERNSTEIN, MARVIN M. *et al.*	*Child Protection Law in Canada*	Crswl (LL)
PHILLIPS, DOUGLAS W.	*Adoption Law in Canada: Practice & Procedure*	Crswl (LL), ceased publication in 2000
WILSON, JEFFREY	*Wilson on Children and the Law*	LN/B (LL)
PAYNE, JULIEN D., Q.C., AND MARILYN A. PAYNE	*Canadian Family Law*, 3d ed	Irwin 2008
ROY, ALAIN	*Le droit de l'adoption au Québec*	W & LaF 2006
LAVALLÉE, CARMEN	*L'enfant, ses familles et les institutions de l'adoption : regards sur le droit français et le droit québécois*	W & LaF 2005
FODDEN, SIMON R.	*Family Law*	Irwin 1999
BERNSTEIN, MARVIN M., AND LYNN M. KIRWIN	*Child Protection: Practice & Procedure*	Crswl 1996

4.

ADVERTISING LAW

This is a subtopic that touches upon a number of others, including: COMMERCIAL LAW, COMMUNICATIONS LAW, INTELLECTUAL PROPERTY LAW, TRADE-MARKS. Most of these areas are within the purview of the federal government.

PUBLICITÉ COMMERCIALE

Ce sujet traite des divers aspects de la publicité commerciale et des supports autorisés. La majorité des ouvrages portant sur le droit de la protection du CONSOMMATEUR aborde la publicité. Certains aspects non-commerciaux relevant de lois particulières (élections, affichage, etc.).

PRITCHARD, BRENDA, AND KATE HENDERSON	*The Source*	Institute of Canadian Advertising (LL)
YOUNG, DAVID M.W., AND BRIAN R. FRASER	*Canadian Advertising & Marketing Law*	Crswl (LL)
PRITCHARD, BRENDA, AND SUSAN VOGT	*Advertising and Marketing Law in Canada*, 2d ed.	LN/B 2006
L'HEUREUX, NICOLE	*Droit de la consommation*, 5e éd.	Y Blais 2000
DIMOCK, RONALD E. *et al.*	*Canadian Marketing Law Handbook*	Crswl 1991

5.

ADVOCACY

This subject deals with the skills of legal oratory and rhetoric. There is a wealth of material providing advice on how to prepare and deliver an effective legal argument. Most of these impart suggestions with regard to research, legal reasoning, drafting of pleadings, client counselling, and presentation in court. Related topics: LEGAL REASONING, LEGAL RESEARCH, LEGAL WRITING.

ART DE LA PLAIDOIRIE

Ce sujet traite de l'éloquence et de la rhétorique juridiques. La plupart des ouvrages couvrent la recherche des arguments, le raisonnement, la rédaction des plaidoiries, l'opinion juridique et la présentation devant le tribunal. Voir aussi : RECHERCHE DOCUMENTAIRE et RÉDACTION JURIDIQUE.

OLAH, JOHN A.	*The Art and Science of Advocacy*	Crswl (LL)
STUESSER, LEE	*An Advocacy Primer*, 3d ed.	Crswl 2005
ADAIR, GEOFFREY D.E.	*On Trial: Advocacy Skills, Law, and Practice*, 2d ed.	LN/B 2004
SALHANY, ROGER E.	*Preparation and Presentation of a Civil Action*	LN/B 2000
WHITE, ROBERT B., Q.C.	*The Art of Trial*	CLB 1993

◆ AÉRIEN (DROIT) voir AVIATION & AERONAUTICS LAW

6.

AGENCY

Agency is a contractual or legal relationship, often fiduciary in nature, in which one party (the agent) agrees to act on behalf of the interests of another (the principal). It is often also dealt with in other areas. Related topics: COMMERCIAL LAW, CONTRACTS, TRUSTS.

MANDAT

Un des contrats nommés prévus au *Code civil*. Le mandat s'étend également au droit des affaires, aux personnes (*cf.* mandat en cas d'inaptitude) et fait partie intégrante de nombreux contrats d'enterprise ou de service.

BILLINS, ROGER	*Agency Law* (U.K.)	S & M (LL)
BARREAU DU QUÉBEC	*Obligations et recours contre un curateur, tuteur ou mandataire défaillant 2008*	Y Blais 2008
HARVEY, CAMERON	*Agency Law Primer,* 3d ed.	Crswl 2003
CANTIN CUMYN, MADELEINE	*L'administration du bien d'autrui*	Y Blais 2000
LAMONTAGNE, DENYS-CLAUDE ET BERNARD LAROCHELLE	*Droit spécialisé des contrats*	Y Blais 1999
FRIDMAN, GERALD HENRY LOUIS	*Fridman's Law of Agency,* 7th ed.	LN/B 1996
FRIDMAN, GERALD HENRY LOUIS	"Agency" in vol. 1, title 4 of *Canadian Encyclopedic Digest* (Ontario) & (Western)	Crswl 1996
CANADIAN BAR ASSOCIATION — ONTARIO	*Business Law: Law of Agency*	CBA Ontario, Continuing Legal Education 1992

AGRICULTURAL & AQUACULTURE LAW

This topic deals with the law as it relates to the production of various foodstuffs. It covers a number of subtopics, including COMMERCIAL LAW, CONTRACTS, ENVIRONMENTAL LAW, MUNICIPAL LAW, NUISANCE, REAL PROPERTY, TAXATION. These matters are mostly dealt with in the provincial sphere.

AGRICULTURE ET CULTURE HYDROPONIQUE

Domaine longtemps sous-développé du droit des BIENS ET PROPRIÉTÉ et naguère confiné aux questions civilistes, le droit de l'agriculture et culture hydroponique émerge de plus en plus comme un domaine nouveau du droit public (zonage agricole, aménagement et urbanisme, protection de l'ENVIRONNEMENT) et du droit du CONSOMMATEUR (aliments). La question de la protection juridique des obtentions végétales relève des BREVETS. Pour les subventions dans le cadre de l'*ALENA*, voir ce sujet.

MUNRO, G., AND K. OELSCHLAGEL	*Taxation of Farmers and Fishermen*	Crswl (LL)
LABRECQUE, PIERRE ET CLAUDE RÉGNIER	*Loi sur la mise en marché des produits agricoles, alimentaires et de la pêche : les règles juridiques applicables à la production et à la mise en marché collective au Québec*	Y Blais 2006
FULLER, ROBERT S., AND DONALD E. BUCKINGHAM	*Agriculture Law in Canada*	LN/B 1999
LYMAN, SHERMAN, JEAN-E. BRASSARD, AND ELIZABETH PORTMAN	"Agriculture" in vol. 1A, title 5 of *Canadian Encyclopedic Digest* (Ontario)	Crswl 1998
BENON, MARJORIE L.	*Agricultural Law in Canada 1867–1995: With Particular Reference to Saskatchewan*	Canadian Institute of Resources Law, U of Cgy 1996
WILDSMITH, BRUCE H.	*Aquaculture: The Legal Framework*	EM 1982

♦ ALENA (*ACCORD DE LIBRE-ÉCHANGE NORD-AMÉRICAIN*) voir *NAFTA* (*NORTH AMERICAN FREE TRADE AGREEMENT*)

8.

ALTERNATIVE DISPUTE RESOLUTION (ADR)

Alternative dispute resolution (ADR) is the resolution of disputes through means other than litigation. The most common alternatives are arbitration and mediation. The high expense and excessive length of time required for traditional litigation have led to an enormous increase in the use of ADR in settling legal disputes. It is a practice that is highly encouraged (and in some cases mandated) by Canadian courts. Related topics: CIVIL PROCEDURE, COMMERCIAL ARBITRATION.

MODES ALTERNATIFS DE RÉSOLUTION DES CONFLITS (MARC)

La résolution des conflits par des moyens autres que le procès. Les solutions de rechange les plus communes sont l'arbitrage et la médiation. Le coût élevé et la durée excessive du procès traditionnel ont mené à une grande augmentation de l'utilisation des méthodes alternatives de règlement des différends. Les tribunaux canadiens encouragent fortement cette pratique. Voir aussi : PROCÉDURE CIVILE et ARBITRAGE (CIVIL ET COMMERCIAL).

FISHER, G., AND ALLAN J. STITT	*Alternative Dispute Resolution Practice Manual*	CCH Cdn (LL)
SANDERSON, JOHN P., AND RICHARD MACLAREN	*Innovative Dispute Resolution: The Alternative*	Crswl (LL)
CHORNENKI, GENEVIEVE, AND CHRISTINE HART	*Bypass Court: A Dispute Resolution Handbook*, 3d ed.	LN/B 2005
NELSON, ROBERT M.	*Nelson on ADR*	Crswl 2003
PIRIE, ANDREW	*Alternative Dispute Resolution*	Irwin 2000
THIBAULT, JOËLLE	*Les procédures de règlement amiable des litiges au Canada*	W & LaF 2000
BOULLE, LAURENCE, AND KATHLEEN KELLY	*Mediation: Principles, Process, Practice*	LN/B 1998

- AMÉNAGEMENT ET URBANISME voir MUNICIPAL LAW
- ARBITRAGE (CIVIL ET COMMERCIAL) voir COMMERCIAL ARBITRATION ; ALTERNATIVE DISPUTE RESOLUTION (ADR)
- ASSURANCES voir INSURANCE LAW
- AUTEUR (DROIT D') voir COPYRIGHT
- AUTOCHTONES voir ABORIGINAL LAW

9.

AVIATION & AERONAUTICS LAW

This topic comprises aspects of administrative law and transportion law. It is somewhat complex in that it falls, on the one hand, into federal competency (in that it frequently involves interprovincial and international operation), but it is also a provincial matter when it deals with purely local transport. Ultimately, however, this topic is greatly informed by a number of related international conventions to which Canada is a signatory. See also TRANSPORTATION LAW.

AÉRIEN (DROIT)

Le droit aérien comporte des aspects de droit ADMINISTRATIF et de droit des TRANSPORTS. Ce qui le rend complexe, c'est, d'une part, le partage des compétences fédérales (interprovincial et international) et provinciales (transport local) et, d'autre part, le recours au droit international. Le transport aérien repose principalement sur de grandes conventions internationales (dont celle dite « de Varsovie ») auxquelles le Canada a adhéré.

CANADA	*Air Regulations & Aeronautics Act*	Transport Canada (LL)
McCLEAN, J.D. *et al.*	*Shawcross and Beaumont, Air Law*, 4th ed.	LN/B (LL) U.K.
HOLDING, JOHN	*Canadian Manual of International Air Carriage*	Irwin 2005
CANADA	*Aeronautics Act*	Transport Canada 1998
GRAHAM, J. SANDERSON	"Aviation and Air Law" in vol 1A, title 12 of *Canadian Encyclopedic Digest* (Ontario) and vol. 2, title 12 of *Canadian Encyclopedic Digest* (Western)	Crswl 1997
MATTESCO-MATTE, NICOLAS	*Space Activities and Emerging International Law*	McGill Institute of Air & Space Law 1986
MATTESCO-MATTE, NICOLAS	*Traité de droit aérien-aéronautique*, 3e éd.	McGill Institute of Air & Space Law 1980
PAQUETTE, RICHARD	*La responsabilité en droit aérien canadien*	W & LaF 1979

BANKING LAW

Regulated by the federal *Bank Act*, this is an area of almost exclusive federal jurisdiction. However, credit unions and caisses-populaires are creatures of provincial statute, leading to some confusion and blurring of jurisdictions. It is a complex area of the law touching on issues such as responsibilities and obligations of bank officers and directors, rules related to record-keeping, loans and their securities, etc. Related topics: BILLS OF EXCHANGE, COMMERCIAL LAW, DEBTOR & CREDITOR.

BANCAIRE (DROIT)

Le droit des banques appartient d'emblée au droit des *AFFAIRES*. Il couvre la réglementation des activités des banques entre elles et de leurs relations avec la banque centrale. Domaine de compétence fédérale, on y traite parfois des institutions financières analogues de compétence provinciale (caisses d'épargne, caisses populaire et de crédit). Les banques et la monnaie ainsi que le chèque et les *LETTRES DE CHANGE* relèvent du droit fédéral.

TEOLIS, JOHN W., AND C. DAWN JETTEN	Bank Act: *Legislation and Commentary*	LN/B (LL)
OGILVIE, M.H.	*Bank and Customer Law in Canada*	Irwin 2007
L'HEUREUX, NICOLE, EDITH FORTIN ET MARC LACOURSIÈRE	*Droit bancaire*, 4e éd.	Y Blais 2004
DAVID, GUY, AND LOUISE S. PELLY	*Annotated* Bank Act, 2000	Crswl 2000
MANZER, ALISON, AND JORDAN BERNAMOFF	*The Corporate Counsel Guide to Banking & Credit Relationships*	CLB 1999
OGILVIE, M.H.	*Canadian Banking Law*, 2d ed.	Crswl 1998
BAXTER, IAN F.G.	*Law of Banking*, 4th ed.	Crswl 1992

II.

BANKRUPTCY & INSOLVENCY

Controlled by the *Bankruptcy and Insolvency Act*, this is exclusively a federal matter. An insolvent debtor's assets and debts are administered by a third party (a trustee in bankruptcy). A bankrupt is normally deprived of some legal rights until such time as the bankruptcy is discharged (i.e., concluded). Related topics: DEBTOR & CREDITOR, PERSONAL PROPERTY SECURITY.

FAILLITE ET INSOLVABILITÉ

Domaine de plus en plus important du droit des AFFAIRES. La législation y touchant est de compétence fédérale. Curieusement, il souffre de sous-développement doctrinal. La législation a été considérablement remaniée ces dernières années. Ici, comme en DIVORCE, se pose le problème de l'interface avec les notions civilistes du *Code civil du Québec*.

BOUCHER, BERNARD	*Faillite et insolvabilité : une perspective québécoise de la jurisprudence canadienne*	Crswl (FM)
WOOD, RODERICK	*Bankruptcy & Insolvency*	Irwin 2009
BENNETT, FRANK	*Bennett on Bankruptcy*, 9th ed.	CCH Cdn 2008
HOULDEN, LLOYD W., GEOFFREY B. MORAWETZ, AND JANIS PEARL SARRA	*The Annotated* Bankruptcy and Insolvency Act, *2008*	Crswl 2007
GRUNDY, SUSAN M. *et al.*	*The Insolvency Laws of Canada*	Justis 2006
MCELCHERAN, KEVIN P.	*Commercial Insolvency in Canada*	LN/B 2005
BILODEAU, PAUL-ÉMILE	*Précis de la faillite et de l'insolvabilité*, 2e éd.	CCH 2004
DESLAURIERS, JACQUES	*La faillite et l'insolvabilité au Québec*	W & LaF 2004
ZIEGEL, JACOB S., ANTHONY J. DUGGAN, AND THOMAS G.W. TELFER	*Canadian Bankruptcy and Insolvency Law, Cases, Texts, and Materials*	EM 2003
HOULDEN, LLOYD W., AND GEOFFREY B. MORAWETZ	*Bankruptcy and Insolvency Law of Canada*, 3d ed.	Crswl 1989

- BIENS ET PROPRIÉTÉ voir PROPERTY; REAL PROPERTY

BILLS OF EXCHANGE

A subset of both commercial law and banking law, this area of law, which includes cheques, promissory notes, and negotiable instruments, will undergo considerable internationalization under the influence of international commercial law. The United Nations Commission for International Trade Law (UNCITRAL) undertakes works in this domain. Jurisdictionally, this is a federal matter.

LETTRES DE CHANGE

Domaine stable du droit des AFFAIRES et sous-ensemble du droit BANCAIRE, les lettres de change – qui englobent le chèque et le billet à ordre – connaîtront une plus grande internationalisation sous l'influence du droit COMMERCIAL INTERNATIONAL. La Commission des Nations Unies pour le Droit Commercial International (CNUDCI) mène des travaux en ce sens.

OGILVIE, M.H.	*Bank and Customer Law in Canada*	Irwin 2007
L'HEUREUX, NICOLE, EDITH FORTIN ET MARC LACOURSIÈRE	*Droit bancaire*, 4e éd.	Y Blais 2004
CRAWFORD, BRADLEY, Q.C.	*Payment, Clearing, and Settlement in Canada*	CLB 2002
ASTER, LEORA, AND LAZAR SARNA	*Annotated* Bills of Exchange Act	Jewel Publishers 1999
MANZER, ALISON, AND JORDAN BERNAMOFF	*The Corporate Counsel Guide to Banking & Credit Relationships*	CLB 1999
OGILVIE, M.H.	*Canadian Banking Law*, 2d ed.	Crswl 1998
BAXTER, IAN F.G.	*Law of Banking*, 4th ed.	Crswl 1992

13.

BIOETHICS

Considered to be at the crossroads of ethical questions related to life and death, bioethics raises two difficulties for lawyers as a field of study. On the one hand, ethics are distributed in a variety of fields (e.g., medicine, pharmacy, and other professions); on the other hand, other disciplines intervene (e.g., theology, philosophy, sociology, biology, etc.) so that the lawyer is not the sole decision-maker and is not guided exclusively by matters of law.

BIOÉTHIQUE

Carrefour des questions éthiques liées à la vie et à la mort, la bioéthique, comme champ d'étude, pose deux difficultés aux juristes. D'une part, l'éthique se trouve répartie dans une foule d'aspects ou de domaines éclatés (médecine, pharmacie, déontologie professionnelle) ; d'autre part, d'autres disciplines interviennent sur les problèmes (théologie, philosophie, sociologie, biologie, etc.), ne laissant plus le juriste seul à décider. Les problèmes particuliers du consentement aux soins sont réglés au Code civil et souvent abordés dans les ouvrages traitant de la PERSONNE ou de la SANTÉ – MÉDECINE.

BLANCHARD, ADRIENNE M., AND JANE B.H. STEINBERG,	*Life Sciences Law in Canada*	Crswl (LL) 2006
BARAKETT, RAYMOND	*Précis annoté de la Loi sur les services de santé et les services sociaux, 4e éd.*	Y Blais 2004
MARSHALL, DAVID T.	*The Law of Human Experimentation*	LN/B 2000
KNOPPERS, BARTHA MARIA, TIMOTHY CAULFIELD, AND T. DOUGLAS KINSELLA, eds.	*Legal Rights and Human Genetic Material*	EM 1996
ONTARIO LAW REFORM COMMISSION	*Report on Genetic Testing*	OLRC 1996
BERNARD, CLAIRE, BARTHA MARIA KNOPPERS, AND LADAN NASSIRY	*Legal Aspects of Research and Clinical Practice with Human Beings*	National Council on Bioethics in Human Research 1992

14.

CHARITIES & CHARITABLE CORPORATIONS

An ever burgeoning area of the law, it deals with a variety of legal matters as they relate to charities, charitable corporations and organizations, and often non-profit corporations. These are governed by both federal (e.g., incorporation, taxation) and provincial law. Related topics: COMMERCIAL LAW, CORPORATE LAW, GAMING & LOTTERIES.

ORGANISMES DE BIENFAISANCE

Ce secteur en plein développement couvre principalement les aspects fiscaux des activités dites charitables et à buts non lucratifs. On peut y rattacher la FISCALITÉ et les JEUX ET LOTERIES.

DRACHE, ARTHUR B.C., Q.C.	Canadian Taxation of Charities and Donations	Crswl (LL)
DRACHE, ARTHUR B.C., Q.C.	The Charity & Not-for-Profit Sourcebook: Cases, Legislation, & Commentary	Crswl (LL)
HOFFSTEIN, MARIA ELENA, TERRANCE S. CARTER, AND ADAM M. PARACHIN	Charities Legislation and Commentary, 2008	LN/B 2007
BOURGEOIS, DONALD J.	The Law of Charitable and Not-for-Profit Organizations, 3d ed.	LN/B 2002
BOURGEOIS, DONALD J.	The Law of Charitable & Casino Gaming	LN/B 1999

- *CHARTER OF RIGHTS AND FREEDOMS* see HUMAN RIGHTS AND THE *CHARTER OF RIGHTS AND FREEDOMS*
- *CHARTE DES DROITS* voir HUMAN RIGHTS AND THE *CHARTER OF RIGHTS AND FREEDOMS*

15.

CHILDREN AND THE LAW

Often treated as a subtopic within family law, this area dealing with legal minors is actually somewhat broader and has connections with criminal law and tort *inter alia*. In an environment that is becoming more sensitive to the legal rights of children, this is increasingly becoming a more active area of research and litigation. Related topics: ABORIGINAL LAW, ADOPTION, CRIMINAL LAW, DIVORCE, EDUCATION LAW, FAMILY LAW, HUMAN RIGHTS AND THE *CHARTER OF RIGHTS AND FREEDOMS*, TORTS, YOUNG OFFENDERS.

JEUNESSE

Ce domaine regroupe l'ensemble des questions juridiques de la jeunesse au plan civil, ce qui comprend les divers régimes de protection. Certains aspects sont évidemment abordés avec le droit de la FAMILLE ou de la personne. L'aspect CRIMINEL ou pénal est abordé sous JEUNES CONTREVENANTS.

WILSON, JEFFREY	*Wilson on Children and the Law*	LN/B (LL)
LE MAY, SYLVIE	*La minorité et la tutelle (Art. 153 à 255 C.c.Q.) : commentaires sur le* Code civil du Québec	Y Blais 2007
ROCK, NORA	*Child Protection and Canadian Law: A Service Perspective*	EM 2005
TÉTRAULT, MICHEL	*Droit de la famille*, 3e éd.	Y Blais 2005
ZUKER, JUSTICE MARVIN A., RANDOLPH C. HAMMOND, AND RODERICK C. FLYNN	*Children's Law Handbook*	Crswl 2005
BALA, NICK, ed.	*Canadian Child Welfare Law*, 2d ed.	Crswl 2004
MALESZYK, ANNE	*Crimes Against Children*	CLB 2004

16.

CIVIL CODE OF QUÉBEC

The basis of most areas of private law in the province of Québec is the *Civil Code of Québec*, which came into effect in 1994 and grew out of the *Civil Code of Lower Canada*, which was enacted in 1865 and came into force and effect in 1866, prior to the Canadian confederation. It is comprised of ten "books" (major subject areas) and over three thousand specific sections (articles). Most versions are written in both French and English.

CODE CIVIL DU QUÉBEC

Nous ne donnons ici que les publications d'ensemble sur le nouveau *Code civil du Québec*, entré en vigueur le 1er janvier 1994. Les principales parties du Code font l'objet d'une rubrique de cette publication. Le contenu spécifique de l'une ou l'autre de ces publications est également rappelé sous l'une ou l'autre des rubriques lorsque jugé utile. La panoplie des ressources documentaires disponibles pour l'étude du nouveau Code s'étend des plus lointaines racines de l'ancien droit français jusqu'aux plus volatiles conjugaisons des versions électroniques.

CÔTÉ, PIERRE-ANDRÉ ET DANIEL JUTRAS	*Le droit transitoire civil – sources annotées*	Y Blais (FM)
BAUDOUIN, JEAN-LOUIS ET YVON RENAUD	Code civil du Québec *annoté (versions électroniques disponibles de la SOQUIJ)*	W & LaF [annuel]
LE MAY, DENIS	*The* Civil Code of Quebec *in Chart Form*	Irwin 2006
BARREAU DU QUÉBEC ET CHAMBRE DES NOTAIRES	*La réforme du* Code civil*; Tome 1: Personnes, successions et biens; Tome 2: Obligations, contrats nommés; Tome 3: Priorités et hypothèques, preuve et prescription, publicité des droits, droit international privé, dispositions transitoires*	Barreau du Québec 1993
BRIERLEY, JOHN E.C., AND RODERICK A. MACDONALD	*Quebec Civil Law: An Introduction to Quebec Private Law*	EM 1993
FACULTÉ DE DROIT, UNIVERSITÉ DE MONTRÉAL	*Le nouveau* Code civil*: interprétation et application: les journées Maximilien-Caron, 1992*	Thémis 1993
QUÉBEC, MINISTÈRE DE LA JUSTICE	*Le* Code civil du Québec*: un mouvement de société*	Publications Québec 1993
LE MAY, DENIS	*Le* Code civil du Québec *en tableaux synoptiques*	W & LaF 1992

17.

CIVIL PROCEDURE

This deals with the various rules of court of the federal and provincial courts. These rules mandate the manner in which legal disputes may be brought forward and resolved in a court of law. The rules are articulated in regulations pursuant to both provincial and federal legislation. Related topics: CLASS ACTIONS, COURTS, EVIDENCE (CIVIL).

PROCÉDURE CIVILE

Ce domaine a connu de nombreux ajustements suite à l'entrée en vigueur du nouveau *Code civil*. Si les principes supplétifs se trouvent dans le droit français, rappelons qu'une partie de la procédure provient du droit anglo-américain ; la procédure serait un domaine « mixte ».

CUDMORE, GORDON D.	*Choate on Discovery*, 2d ed.	Crswl (LL)
HUGHES, ROGER T.	*Federal Court of Canada Service*	LN/B (LL)
WILLISTON, W.B., R.J. ROLLS, AND BERKLEY D. SELLS	*Williston & Rolls Ontario Court Forms*, 2d ed.	LN/B (LL)
STOCKWOOD, DAVID, Q.C.	*Civil Litigation: A Practical Handbook*, 5th ed.	Crswl 2004
FERLAND, DENIS	*Précis de procédure civile du Québec*, 4e éd.	Y Blais 2003
REID, HUBERT	*La réforme du Code de procédure civile*	W & LaF 2002
ORKIN, MARK M.	*The Law of Costs*, 2d ed.	CLB 2001
BRISSON, JEAN-MAURICE	*La formation d'un droit mixte : l'évolution de la procédure civile de 1774 à 1867*	Thémis 1986

18.

CLASS ACTIONS

Once very rare in Canada, litigation by mass plaintiffs is becoming increasingly common (particularly in areas such as products liability and securities). The court rules of the provinces and federal courts dictate the ways and means by which multiple litigants can launch class action lawsuits in their jurisdictions. Related topics: CIVIL PROCEDURE, NEGLIGENCE, NUISANCE, PRODUCTS LIABILITY, SECURITIES, TORTS.

RECOURS COLLECTIF

Cette PROCÉDURE CIVILE, inscrite au *Code de procédure civile*, permet d'intenter un recours au nom d'un groupe de personnes. Voir aussi : CONSOMMATEUR et RESPONSABILITÉ CIVILE.

BRANCH, WARD	*Class Actions in Canada*	CLB (LL)
EIZENGA, MICHAEL A. *et al.*	*Class Actions Law & Practice*	LN/B (LL)
HAMER, DAVID I., AND ELIZABETH STEWART	*Defending Class Actions in Canada*, 2d ed.	CCH Cdn 2007
LAFOND, PIERRE-CLAUDE	*Le recours collectif, le rôle du juge et sa conception de la justice : impact et évolution*	Y Blais 2006
PITEL, STEPHEN A., ed.	*Litigating Conspiracy: An Analysis of Competition Class Actions*	Irwin 2006
CASSELS, JAMIE, AND CRAIG JONES	*The Law of Large-Scale Claims: Product Liability, Mass Torts, and Complex Litigation in Canada*	Irwin 2005
JONES, CRAIG	*The Theory of Class Actions*	Irwin 2003
LAUZON, YVES	*Le recours collectif*	Y Blais 2001
MARAGH, KATHLEEN	"Judgments on Counterclaims, Crossclaims, Third Party Claims, and in Class Actions," Part IV of "Judgments and Orders" in vol. 20, title 82 of the *Canadian Encyclopedic Digest* (Western)	Crswl 2000

- *CODE CIVIL DU QUÉBEC* voir *CIVIL CODE OF QUÉBEC*

19.

COMMERCIAL ARBITRATION

Disputes between commercial entities are often resolved by reference to third-party arbitrators. These works deal with the conventions employed in such arbitral exercises. If one party to such a commercial dispute is the federal government, then the *Commercial Arbitration Act* is applied. Related topics: COMMERCIAL LAW, CONTRACTS, INTERNATIONAL SALE OF GOODS.

ARBITRAGE (CIVIL ET COMMERCIAL)

Le *Code civil* comprend maintenant des dispositions relatives à l'arbitrage tant civil que commercial, tant internes qu'internationales. Ces dispositions s'inspirent de la loi uniforme de la Commission des Nations Unies pour le Droit Commercial International (CNUDCI).

EARLE, WENDY J.	*Drafting ADR & Arbitration Clauses for Commercial Contracts*	Crswl (LL)
SANDERSON, JOHN P., AND RICHARD MACLAREN	*Innovative Dispute Resolution: The Alternative*	Crswl (LL)
STITT, ALLAN J., ed.	*Alternative Dispute Resolution Practice Manual*	CCH Cdn (LL)
BACHAND, FRÉDÉRIC	*L'intervention du juge canadien avant et durant un arbitrage commercial international*	Y Blais 2005
MACEWAN, J. KENNETH, AND LUDMILA BARBARA HERBST	*Commercial Arbitration in Canada: A Guide to Domestic and International Arbitrations*	CLB 2004
NEUFELD, ROXANNE	"International Commercial Arbitration and Foreign Arbitral Awards," in Part V of "Arbitration," in vol. 1A, title 18, paragraphs 552–80 in *Canadian Encyclopedic Digest* (Ontario) and in vol. 2, title 8 of the *Canadian Encyclopedic Digest* (Western)	Crswl 2004

COMMERCIAL LAW

This is a vast area that might also be termed "Business Law." It deals with matters of conducting commercial enterprises in Canada. Titles listed under this heading will be more general and omnibus in scope. More specific aspects of commercial law are covered in other headings: BANKING LAW, BANKRUPTCY & INSOLVENCY, COMPETITION LAW, CONSUMER PROTECTION LAW, CORPORATE LAW, FRANCHISING, INTERNATIONAL SALE OF GOODS, PARTNERSHIPS, PRODUCTS LIABILITY, SALE OF GOODS, SECURITIES, TAXATION.

AFFAIRES (DROIT DES)

Vaste domaine couvrant plus de la moitié des branches du droit. On utilise cette expression pour désigner l'ensemble des dimensions juridiques applicables à la conduite des affaires (« *doing business* »). L'expression « droit commercial » tend à disparaître avec le nouveau *Code civile du Québec*. Plusieurs aspects du droit des affaires font l'objet d'une rubrique distincte : BANCAIRE (DROIT) ; COMMERCIAL INTERNATIONAL (DROIT) ; COMPAGNIES ; CONCURRENCE (DROIT DE LA) ; FAILLITE ET INSOLVABILITÉ ; FRANCHISE ; LETTRES DE CHANGE ; VALEURS MOBILIÈRES. Il s'ensuit que tout ouvrage qui porte sur l'ensemble du droit des affaires ne peut être considéré que comme une introduction.

BABE, JENNIFER E. *et al.*	*Canadian Commercial Law Guide*	CCH Cdn (LL)
BEATTIE, ROBERT W. *et al.*	*The Directors Manual*	CCH Cdn (LL)
ANTAKI, NABIL *et al.*	*Droit et pratique de l'enterprise*, 2e éd.	Y Blais 2007
McGUINNESS, KEVIN P.	*Law & Practice of Canadian Business Corporations*, 2d ed.	LN/B 2007
LACASSE, NICOLE	*Droit de l'entreprise*, 6e éd.	Narval 2006
REITER, BARRY	*Directors' Duties in Canada*, 3d ed.	CCH Cdn 2006
LUSTGARTEN, LIONEL S., NICK PAPATHEODORAKOS, AND MILTON W. WINSTON	*Essentials of Québec business law*, 2d ed.	Bensar Commerce 2003
REITER, BARRY, AND MELANIE SHISHLER	*Joint Ventures: Legal & Business Perspectives*	Irwin 1999

♦ COMMERCIAL INTERNATIONAL (DROIT) voir INTERNATIONAL SALE OF GOODS ; INTERNATIONAL TRADE LAW

COMMUNICATIONS LAW

This area of law is almost entirely federal in scope and deals with telecommunications, broadcasting, and matters related to print media as well. Related topics: ADVERTISING LAW, COMMERCIAL LAW, CONSTITUTIONAL LAW, COPYRIGHT, ENTERTAINMENT & SPORTS LAW, INTELLECTUAL PROPERTY LAW, PRIVACY LAW & ACCESS TO INFORMATION.

COMMUNICATIONS (DROIT DES)

Vaste domaine relativement peu développé qui couvre les moyens de communication (radio, télévision, téléphone, presse écrite), les entreprises qui les possèdent, leurs activités et le contenu qu'ils véhiculent. Domaine maintenant presque exclusivement de compétence fédérale, sauf certains aspects complémentaires (par ex. responsabilité des journalistes, etc.). Les aspects de censure sont traités par le biais des libertés d'expression et d'information prévues aux chartes des droits. Certains aspects relèvent du domaine CRIMINEL (libelle, méfait, propagande haineuse, etc.), d'autres touchent aux aspects civils de la protection de la vie privée (personnes (droit des) ; ACCÈS À L'INFORMATION).

DUARTE, TONY	*Canadian Film & Television Business & Legal Practice*	CLB (LL)
JOHNSTON, DAVID, *et al.*	*Communications Law in Canada*	LN/B (LL)
RYAN, MICHAEL H.	*Canadian Telecommunications Law & Regulation Guide*	Crswl (LL)
BRECHER, JAY	"Media and Postal Communications," a vol. of *Halsbury's Laws of Canada*, 1st ed.	LN/B 2007
HANDA, SUNNY *et al.*	"Communications," a vol. of *Halsbury's Laws of Canada*, 1st ed.	LN/B 2007
JOBB, DEAN	*Media Law for Canadian Journalists*	EM 2006
BEAUCHAMP, LOUIS	*L'avocat et les médias*	Y Blais 2005
MORISSETTE, RODOLPHE	*La presse et les tribunaux: un mariage de raison*, 2e éd.	W & LaF 2004
MARTIN, ROBERT	*Media Law*, 2d ed.	Irwin 2003

COMPETITION LAW

This is a matter of primarily federal jurisdiction (by way of the *Competition Act* which aims at preventing anti-competitive behaviours by Canadian businesses). Competition policy, as set by the federal Parliament, is driven primarily by concepts of "fairness" in the marketplace, but also by the desire to achieve economic efficiency and adaptability. Related topics: COMMERCIAL LAW, CORPORATE LAW, PARTNERSHIPS. This area of law is sometimes referred to as "Antitrust law."

CONCURRENCE (DROIT DE LA)

Domaine de compétence fédérale destiné à contrer l'établissement de monopoles jugés nuisibles à une saine économie libérale. Il s'agit d'une loi pénale tout autant que régulatrice. Certains aspects du droit fédéral de la protection du CONSOMMATEUR s'y retrouvent.

ADDY, GEORGE N., AND WILLIAM L. VANVEEN	*Competition Law Service*	CLB (LL)
AFFLECK, DON, AND WAYNE MCCRACKEN	*Canadian Competition Law*	Crswl (LL)
FACEY, BRIAN A., AND DANY H. ASSAF	*Competition & Antitrust Law: Canada & The United States*, 3d ed.	LN/B 2006
LAVERY, DE BILLY	*Manuel de droit de la concurrence : lois annotées, analyse, commentaires*	Y Blais 2004
FLAVELL, C. J. MICHAEL, AND CHRISTOPHER J. KENT	*Canadian Competition Law Handbook*	Crswl 1997
MUNGOVAN, MICHAEL O'DEA	*Competition Law: A Legal Handbook for Business*	LN/B 1990

CONFLICT OF LAWS

It is not uncommon for a legal dispute among private parties to involve the laws of different legal systems, for example, motor vehicle accidents involving Canadian cars in American states, or contracts of sale undertaken in other jurisdictions. In these cases, Canadian courts look to a set of rules that assist them in resolving such disputes. It should be noted that, as a legal matter, conflict of laws is different from international law, although many of the same issues arise within both. Related topic: PRIVATE INTERNATIONAL LAW.

INTERNATIONAL PRIVÉ (DROIT)

Branche importante du droit civil, le nouveau *Code civil du Québec* lui consacre un livre entier (le dixième). La réputation de complexité du DIP en rebute plus d'un, mais la réalité transnationale et internationale moderne le rend inéluctable. Certains aspects commerciaux sont également abordés du point de vue du droit COMMERCIAL INTERNATIONAL.

CASTEL, J.-G.	*Introduction to Conflict of Laws*, 4th ed.	LN/B (LL)
WALKER, JANET	*Castel & Walker: Canadian Conflict of Laws*, 6th ed.	LN/B (LL)
COLLINS, LAWRENCE	*Dicey & Morris: The Conflict of Laws*, 14th ed. (U.K.)	S & M 2006
EMANUELLI, CLAUDE	*Droit international privé québécois*, 2e éd.	W & LaF 2006
WALKER, JANET	"Conflicts of Law," a vol. of *Halsbury's Laws of Canada*, 1st ed.	LN/B 2006
CANADA	*The Harmonization of Federal Legislation with Québec Civil Law and Canadian Bijuralism*	Canada, Department of Justice 2005
JACK, DEBRA L.	"Conflict of Laws" in vol. 4A, title 28 of the *Canadian Encyclopedic Digest* (Ontario) and in vol. 6, title 30 of the *Canadian Encyclopedic Digest* (Western)	Crswl 1997

+ CONGÉDIEMENT voir EMPLOYMENT LAW; LABOUR LAW; WRONGFUL DISMISSAL
+ CONSOMMATEUR voir CONSUMER PROTECTION LAW

24.

CONSTITUTIONAL LAW

These titles deal with the constitutional foundations of Canada as enacted by the *Constitution Act, 1867* (formerly the *British North America Act*). They principally deal with the division of federal and provincial powers and the various criteria for determining jurisdiction in the absence of clear articulation thereon by the Act. These titles do not deal with constitutional civil rights *per se* (for those see HUMAN RIGHTS AND THE *CHARTER OF RIGHTS AND FREEDOMS*). Related topics: ABORIGINAL LAW, LANGUAGE LAW.

CONSTITUTIONNEL (DROIT)

La présence des chartes des droits ne doit pas faire oublier les autres questions de droit public fondamental, la structure et le fonctionnement des organes de l'État et le partage des compétences législatives entre les parlements du pays. Tous les problèmes remontent d'une manière ou d'une autre au droit constitutionnel (par ex. la question du territoire canadien, le statut juridique du MILITAIRE, etc.).

BRUN, HENRI	*Droit constitutionnel*, 5e éd.	Y Blais 2008
DUPLÉ, NICOLE	*Droit constitutionnel : principes fondamentaux*, 3e éd.	W & LaF 2007
HOGG, PETER	*Constitutional Law of Canada*, 5th ed.	Crswl 2007
MONAHAN, PATRICK J.	*Constitutional Law*, 3d ed.	Irwin 2006
FORCESE, CRAIG, AND AARON FREEMAN	*The Laws of Government: The Legal Foundations of Canadian Democracy*	Irwin 2005
FUNSTON, BERNARD W., AND EUGENE MEEHAN	*Canada's Constitutional Law in a Nutshell*, 3d ed.	Crswl 2003
CANADIAN CONSTITUTIONAL LAW GROUP	*Canadian Constitutional Law*, 3d ed.	EM 2002
TREMBLAY, ANDRÉ	*Droit constitutionnel, principes*, 2e éd.	Thémis 2000
BAUDOIN, GÉRALD A.	*La constitution du Canada : insitutions, partage des pouvoirs, droits et libertés*	W & LaF 1991
FINKELSTEIN, NEIL R.	*Laskin's Canadian Constitutional Law*, 5th ed.	Crswl 1986

25.

CONSTRUCTION LAW

Construction law concerns the law as it relates to the various issues surrounding the design and construction of buildings. This is often a complicated area of litigation in that it frequently involves numerous contractors and sub-contractors, etc. For the most part, this is a subject informed by provincial law. There are numerous provincial builders' or construction liens statutes that provide some statutory protections for builders and dictate the manner in which remedies may be sought.

CONSTRUCTION (DROIT)

Domaine du droit privé où il resterait confiné si ce n'était des nombreuses réglementations relatives aux conditions des CONTRATS ou du TRAVAIL. Le domaine est complexe également en raison des contrats adjugés par l'administration (voir ADMINISTRATIF (DROIT)) ainsi que des systèmes semi-publics d'appel d'offres mis de l'avant par des consortiums d'entrepreneurs.

BRISTOW, DAVID I., AND DOUGLAS W. MACKLEM	*Construction Builders' and Mechanics' Liens in Canada*, 7th ed.	Crswl (LL)
GOLDSMITH, IMMANUEL, AND THOMAS G. HEINTZMAN	*Goldsmith on Canadian Building Contracts*, 4th ed.	Crswl (LL)
GLAHOLT, DUNCAN W., AND MARKUS ROTTERDAM	"Construction," a vol. of *Halsbury's Laws of Canada*, 1st ed.	LN/B 2008
KAUFFMAN, DAVID H.	*The Construction Hypotec*	W & LaF 2007
SILVER, ROBERT, AND GREG T. FURLONG	*Construction Dispute Resolution Handbook*	LN/B 2004
BARREAU DU QUÉBEC	*Développements récents en droit de la construction*	Y Blais 2000
DEMERS, NANCY	*Précis du droit de la construction*	Y Blais 2000
LEFEBVRE, GUY	*L'édification du nouveau droit de la construction : les Journées Maximilien-Caron*	Thémis 2000
KOTT, OLIVIER F. ET CLAUDINE ROY	*La construction au Québec : perspectives juridiques*	W & LaF 1998
KIRSH, HARVEY J., AND LORI A. ROTH	*Kirsh and Roth: The Annotated Construction Contract*	CLB 1997
WALLACE, I. N. DUNCAN, ed.	*Hudson's Building and Engineering Contracts*, 11th ed. (U.K.)	S & M 1995

26.

CONSUMER PROTECTION LAW

A somewhat new area of the law, this area of provincial jurisdiction deals with statutory protections enacted to prevent consumers from falling victim to unfair business practice and to provide them with some measure of remedy should it occur. Related topics: PRODUCTS LIABILITY, SALE OF GOODS.

CONSOMMATEUR (DROIT)

Le consommateur a fait sont entrée au *Code civil du Québec*, mais il demeure bien servi par de nombreuses lois statutaires complémentaires. Domaine de compétence provinciale où le fédéral intervient par des lois particulières de sa compétence (CONCURRENCE (DROIT DE LA), poids et mesures, etc.).

OGILVIE, M.H., ed.	*Consumer Law: Cases and Materials*, 3d ed.	Captus Press 2007
DETURBIDE, MICHAEL	*Consumer Protection Online*	LN/B 2006
McNAUGHTON, ELIZABETH, AND PARNA SABET	*A Guide to the Ontario* Consumer Protection Act, 2007 ed.	LN/B 2006
ROY, PAULINE	*Droit de la protection du consommateur: lois et règlements commentés*	Y Blais 2006
ZIEGEL, JACOB S., AND ANTHONY J. DUGGAN	*Commercial and Consumer Sales Transactions: Cases, Text, and Materials*, 4th ed.	EM 2002
L'HEUREUX, NICOLE	*Droit de la consommation*, 5e éd.	Y Blais 2000
CANADA, WORKING GROUP ON ELECTRONIC COMMERCE AND CONSUMERS	*Principles of Consumer Protection for Electronic Commerce: A Canadian Framework*	Canada, Working Group on Electronic Commerce and Consumers 1999
MASSE, CLAUDE	*Loi sur la protection du consommateur: analyse et commentaires*	Y Blais 1999

27.

CONTRACTS

This ancient area of the law deals primarily with the formation and enforcement of legal agreements between parties. It forms the basis of virtually every type of commercial dealing and is one of few areas of law largely grounded in jurisprudence (caselaw) as opposed to statute, although there are a number of statutes, mostly provincial, which have an impact upon parties' contractual relations. Related topics: COMMERCIAL LAW, INSURANCE LAW, MORTGAGES & LIENS, SALE OF GOODS.

CONTRATS

Domaine du droit privé où il resterait confiné si ce n'était des nombreuses réglementations relatives aux conditions des CONTRATS ou du TRAVAIL. Le domaine est complexe également en raison des contrats adjugés par l'administration (voir : ADMINISTRATIF (DROIT) ainsi que des systèmes semi-publics d'appel d'offres mis de l'avant par des consortiums d'entrepreneurs).

SNYDER, RONALD M., AND HARVIN D. PITCH	*Damages for Breach of Contract*, 2d ed.	Crswl (LL)
LLUELLES, DIDIER	*Droit des obligations*	Thémis 2006
SWAN, ANGELA	*Canadian Contract Law*, 2d ed.	LN/B 2009
DESLAURIERS, JACQUES	*Vente, louage, contrat d'entreprise ou de service*	W & LaF 2005
JOBIN, PIERRE-GABRIEL	*Les obligations*, 6e éd.	Y Blais 2005
MCCAMUS, JOHN	*The Law of Contracts*	Irwin 2005
WADDAMS, STEPHEN M. *et al.*	*Cases and Materials on Contracts*, 3d ed.	EM 2005
WADDAMS, STEPHEN M.	*The Law of Contracts*, 5th ed.	CLB 2005

- CONTRATS INTERNATIONAUX voir CONTRACTS ; INTERNATIONAL SALE OF GOODS ; INTERNATIONAL TRADE LAW
- CONTRATS NOMMÉS voir CONTRACTS
- COPROPRIÉTÉ voir PARTNERSHIPS

28.

COPYRIGHT

This subset of intellectual property deals with the "right to copy" in works of literature, photography, cinema, art, music, etc. Normally, copyright is initially held by the work's creator, but is transferable to certain others. This is an area of specifically federal jurisdiction by way of the *Copyright Act.* Related topics: COMMUNICATIONS LAW, INTELLECTUAL PROPERTY LAW.

AUTEUR (DROIT D')

Jadis réservé à une chapelle de spécialistes, le vaste et complexe domaine de la propriété intellectuelle intéresse de plus en plus de juristes et couvre de plus en plus de dimensions. Du slogan publicitaire à la carte génétique, de la molécule oléophage au circuit informatique, rien n'échappe au nouveau droit de la propriété intellectuelle. Aux branches traditionnelles du domaine – DROIT D'AUTEUR, BREVETS, MARQUES DE COMMERCE et dessin industriel – s'ajoutent maintenant les questions relatives aux circuits informatiques, aux obtentions végétales et à la brevetabilité du vivant en général à l'exclusion des aspects humains, ces derniers relevant de la BIOÉTHIQUE.

RICHARD, HUGUES G., AND LAURENT CARRIÈRE	*Robic Leger Canadian* Copyright Act *Annotated*	Crswl (LL)
HUGHES, ROGER T.	*Copyright Legislation & Commentary, 2008–09* ed.	LN/B 2008
EL KHOURY, PIERRE Y.	*Le fair use et le fair dealing : étude de droit comparé*	Thémis 2007
MOYSE, PIERRE-EMMANUEL	*Le droit de distribution : analyse historique et comparative en droit d'auteur*	Y Blais 2007
TAMARO, NORMAND	*Annotated* Copyright Act, *2007*	Crswl 2007
GENDREAU, YSOLDE, ed.	*Propriété intellectuelle : entre l'art et l'argent / Intellectual Property: Bridging Aesthetics and Economics*	Thémis 2006
GERVAIS, DANIEL J.	*Le droit de la propriété intellectuelle*	Y Blais 2006
TAMARO, NORMAND	*Loi sur le droit d'auteur : texte annoté, 7e éd.*	Crswl 2006
HANDA, SUNNY	*Copyright Law in Canada*	LN/B 2002
VAVER, DAVID	*Copyright Law*	Irwin 2000

29.

CORPORATE LAW

The law as it relates specifically to the creation, governance, operation, and disestablishment of corporations in Canada. This is a matter of mixed jurisdiction in that there is the federal *Canada Business Corporations Act* and there are similar provincial statutes, meaning that a corporation can be incorporated federally or provincially. This topic deals specifically with corporations and not other types of business organizations. Related topics: COMMERCIAL LAW, PARTNERSHIPS.

COMPAGNIES

Domaine traditionnel, bien qu'en constante évolution, le droit des compagnies porte sur l'une des principales formes d'organisation de l'entreprise. C'est une branche importante de droit des AFFAIRES et un domaine de compétence concurrente entre le fédéral et le provincial. Certaines compagnies font l'objet de réglementation particulière (voir : ASSURANCES, BANCAIRE (DROIT)). L'émission d'actions est traitée sous VALEURS MOBILIÈRES. (Rappel : le nouveau *Code civil* comprend un titre entièrement refondu sur la personne morale.)

GROVER, WARREN	*Canada Corporation Manual*	Crswl (LL)
HANSELL, CAROL	*Directors and Officers in Canada: Law and Practice*	Crswl (LL)
MARTEL, PAUL	*Business Corporations in Canada: Legal and Practical Aspects*	Crswl (LL)
PETERSON, DENNIS H.	*Shareholder Remedies in Canada*	LN/B (LL)
CRÊTE, RAYMONDE	*Droit des sociétés par actions : principes fondamentaux*, 2e éd.	Thémis 2008
NICHOLLS, CHRISTOPHER C.	*Mergers, Acquisitions, and Other Changes of Corporate Control*	Irwin 2007
LEFEBVRE, GUY ET STÉPHANE ROUSSEAU	*Introduction au droit des affaires*	Thémis 2006
VAN DUZER, J. ANTHONY	*The Law of Partnerships and Corporations*, 2d ed.	Irwin 2003
MCGUINNESS, KEVIN P.	*The Law and Practice of Canadian Business Corporations*	LN/B 1999

30.

COURTS

This topic lists works related to the court structure of Canada. Courts in Canada are both federal and provincial creations by virtue of sections 96 to 101 (federal courts) and subsection 92(14) (provincial courts) of the *Constitution Act, 1982*. The structure of courts and the rules related to their composition, for example, are anticipated in this topic. Procedures before the courts are dealt with in CIVIL PROCEDURE and CRIMINAL PROCEDURE. See also ADMINISTRATIVE LAW (for information regarding tribunals and commissions), CONSTITUTIONAL LAW.

MAGISTRATURE

Cette rubrique couvre la magistrature comme branche de l'État dans la mesure où elle est étudiée pour elle-même. La production intellectuelle principale des juges, la jurisprudence, est examinée sous l'angle théorique avec les sources de droit. Fait partie de ce domaine, la déontologie judiciaire. Voir aussi : ADMINISTRATIF (DROIT) et CONSTITUTIONNEL (DROIT).

GREENE, IAN	*The Courts*	UBC Press 2006
CANADA	*Canada's Court System*, rev. ed.	Justice Canada 2005
ECCLES, PETER	"Courts" in vol. 9, title 39 of the *Canadian Encyclopedic Digest* (Western)	Crswl 2004
MARAGH, KATHLEEN	"Courts" in vol. 6, title 38 of the *Canadian Encyclopedic Digest* (Ontario)	Crswl 2000
FRIEDLAND, MARTIN L.	*A Place Apart: Judicial Independence and Accountability in Canada*	Canadian Judicial Council 1995
FRIEDLAND, MARTIN L.	*Une place à part : l'indépendance et la responsabilité de la magistrature au Canada*	Conseil canadien de la magistrature 1995
CONSEIL CANADIEN DE LA MAGISTRATURE	*Propos sur la conduite des juges*	Y Blais 1991
RUSSELL, PETER H.	*The Judiciary in Canada: The Third Branch of Government*	McGraw-Hill Ryerson 1987
FRIEDLAND, MARTIN L.	*Courts and Trials: A Multidisciplinary Approach*	U of T Press 1975

31.

CRIMINAL LAW

As Canada's *Criminal Code* is a federal statute, criminal law is considered to be an area of federal jurisdiction. Furthermore, there are other federal criminal enactments (e.g., the *Young Offenders Act*), and quasi-criminal statutes (e.g., the *Canadian Environmental Protection Act*, which contains punitive enforcements provisions). However, there are also numerous quasi-criminal provincial statutes as well (e.g., the various highway traffic codes of the provinces). This topic deals with the non-procedural aspects of Criminal Law. Related topics: CRIMINAL PROCEDURE, ENVIRONMENTAL LAW, EVIDENCE (CRIMINAL), POLICE & PRIVATE SECURITY LAW, SENTENCING, YOUNG OFFENDERS.

CRIMINEL (DROIT)

Branche importante du droit public de compétence fédérale exclusive, le droit criminel s'attache à définir les crimes et prescrit des peines pour leur commission. Les infractions non criminelles, tant fédérales que provinciales, relèvent du droit pénal. La PROCÉDURE PÉNALE, la PREUVE PÉNALE, les SENTENCES et l'emprisonnement, le droit CARCÉRAL font l'objet de rubriques distinctes, même si les plus grands ouvrages de droit criminel embrassent tous ces sujets.

SINCLAIR-PROWSE, JUSTICE JANET A., AND JUSTICE ELIZABETH BENNETT	*Working Manual of Criminal Law*	Crswl (LL)
ROACH, KENT	*Criminal Law*, 4th ed.	Irwin 2009
PARENT, HUGUES	*Traité de droit criminel*	Thémis 2008
GREENSPAN, EDWARD L., AND JUSTICE MARC ROSENBERG	*Martin's Annual Criminal Code, 2007* ed.	CLB 2007
STUART, DON	*Canadian Criminal Law: A Treatise*, 5th ed.	Crswl 2007
WATT, JUSTICE DAVID AND, JUSTICE MICHELLE K. FUERST	*The 2008 Annotated Tremeear's* Criminal Code	Crswl 2007
CÔTÉ-HARPER, GISÈLE	*Traité de droit pénal canadien*, 4e éd.	Y Blais 1998

CRIMINAL PROCEDURE

These are the rules that specify the manner in which a criminal proceeding against an accused must be undertaken. It is an example of "adjective law" as opposed to "substantive law." These rules are spelled out in the federal *Criminal Code* and are significantly informed by a vast body of jurisprudence. Related topics: CRIMINAL PROCEDURE, EVIDENCE (CRIMINAL), YOUNG OFFENDERS.

PROCÉDURE PÉNALE

Branche du droit CRIMINEL et du droit pénal. La procédure est différente selon qu'on est en matière fédérale (droit criminel ou pénal statutaire) ou provinciale (droit statutaire). Voir aussi : SENTENCES.

SALHANY, HON. R.E.	*Canadian Criminal Procedure*, 6th ed.	CLB (LL)
COUGHLAN, STEPHEN	*Criminal Procedure*	Irwin 2008
DELISLE, RON, DON STUART, AND JUSTICE GARY T. TROTTER	*Learning Canadian Criminal Procedure*, 9th ed.	Crswl 2008
BELIVEAU, PIERRE ET MARTIN VAUCLAIR	*Traité général de preuve et de procédure pénales*, 14e éd.	Thémis 2007
LÉTOURNEAU, GILLES	*Code de procédure pénale du Québec annoté*, 4e éd.	Y Blais 2006
PINK, JOEL, AND DAVID PERRIER	*From Crime to Punishment: An Introduction to the Criminal Law System*, 6th ed.	Crswl 2007
ROACH, KENT, JUSTICE GARY T. TROTTER, AND PATRICK HEALEY	*Criminal Law & Procedure: Cases and Materials*, 9th ed.	EM 2004
WEINPER, JUSTICE FERN, AND MARK SANDLER	*Criminal Procedure: Cases, Notes, and Materials*, 2d ed.	LN/B 2003

33.

DAMAGES

In most civil litigation cases, the plaintiff seeks some kind of recompense for the injury suffered. An entire area of law has developed around the awarding of damages and numerous types of awards have developed within this area (e.g., liquidated or unliquidated; general, exemplary, pecuniary, and punitive). This is an area largely grounded in caselaw but informed by various rules of court. Related topics: CIVIL PROCEDURE, REMEDIES & RESTITUTION.

RESPONSABILITÉ CIVILE

Branche majeure du droit civil et partie importante du domaine des OBLIGATIONS.

KLAR, LEWIS N.	*Remedies in Tort*	Crswl (LL)
SNYDER, RONALD M., AND HARVIN D. PITCH	*Damages for Breach of Contract*, 2d ed.	Crswl (LL)
WADDAMS, STEPHEN M.	*The Law of Damages*	CLB (LL)
CASSELS, JAMIE, AND ELIZABETH ADJIN-TETTEY	*Remedies: The Law of Damages*, 2d ed.	Irwin 2008
BEAUDOIN, JEAN-LOUIS ET PATRICE DESLAURIERS	*La responsabilité civile*, 7e éd. (2 vols.) *Principes généraux* (vol. 1) et *Responsabilité professionnelle* (vol. 2)	Y Blais 2007
BARREAU DU QUÉBEC	*Les dommages en matière civile et commerciale*	Y Blais 2006
BARREAU DU QUÉBEC	*Le préjudice corporel*	Y Blais 2006
PERREAULT, JANICK	*L'indemnisation du préjudice corporel des victimes d'accident d'automobile*, 2e éd.	CCH Cdn 2005
BRUCE, CHRISTOPHER	*Assessment of Personal Injury Damages*, 4th ed.	LN/B 2004
GARDNER, DANIEL	*L'évaluation du préjudice corporel*, 2e éd.	Y Blais 2002
COOPER-STEPHENSON, KEN	*Personal Injury Damages in Canada*, 2d ed.	Crswl 1996

34.

DEBTOR & CREDITOR

The law as it relates to persons who owe money (debtors) and those to whom they owe it (creditors). It is different from bankruptcy and insolvency (although they often frequently overlap) in that debtors are not necessarily insolvent. This area is governed by federal and provincial legislation. Related topics: BANKRUPTCY & INSOLVENCY, CONTRACTS, MORTGAGES & LIENS, PERSONAL PROPERTY SECURITY, SALE OF GOODS.

OBLIGATIONS

Cette branche principale du droit civil englobe les CONTRATS, les contrats nommés, une partie du droit applicable au CONSOMMATEUR et la RESPONSABILITÉ CIVILE. Certains de ses aspects font l'objet d'un chapitre distinct : extinction des obligations, restitution des prestations, transmission de l'obligation (subrogation, novation, délégation).

SARNA, LAZAR, AND PHILIP PETRAGLIA	*Annotated Creditors and Debtors Law of Ontario*	LN/B (LL)
TWEEDIE, MICHAEL G.	*Debt Litigation*	CLB (LL)
JOBIN, PIERRE-GABRIEL, JEAN-LOUIS BAUDOUIN ET NATHALIE VÉZINA	*Les Obligations*, 6e éd.	Y Blais 2005
OLIVO, LAURENCE M.	*Debtor-Creditor Law and Procedure*	EM 1999
DUNLOP, C.R.B.	*Creditor-Debtor Law and Procedure*	Crswl 1995
TANCELIN, MAURICE	*Sources des obligations : l'acte juridique légitime*	W & LaF 1993
GERTNER, E. et al.	*Debtor and Creditor Cases and Commentary*, 3d ed.	Crswl 1987

35.

DEFAMATION

Defamation (slander when spoken; libel when written) is a specific tort (cause of action) that is rooted firmly in caselaw. Related topics: COMMUNICATIONS LAW, INTELLECTUAL PROPERTY LAW, PRIVACY LAW & ACCESS TO INFORMATION, TORTS.

DIFFAMATION

La diffamation relève à la fois du droit civil et du droit pénal. Elle peut survenir dans divers contextes liés à la COMMUNICATION, l'ACCÈS À L'INFORMATION et bien entendu la RESPONSABILITÉ CIVILE.

BROWN, RAYMOND E.	*The Law of Defamation in Canada*, 2d ed.	Crswl (LL)
LACROIX, MARIÈVE	*L'avocat diffamateur: ses devoirs de conduite et la mise en œuvre de sa responsabilité civile*	Y Blais 2007
McCONCHIE, ROGER D., AND DAVID A. POTTS	*Canadian Libel and Slander Actions*	Irwin 2004
BROWN, RAYMOND E.	*Defamation Law: A Primer*	Crswl 2003
MACDONALD, CHARLES N.	"Defamation" in vol. 8A, title 45 of the *Canadian Encyclopedic Digest* (Ontario)	Crswl 2000
WILLIAMS, JEREMY S.	*The Law of Libel and Slander in Canada*, 2d ed.	LN/B 1988

• DISCIPLINAIRE (DROIT) voir LEGAL ETHICS; PROFESSIONAL RESPONSIBILITY

36.

DIVORCE

This particular subset of family law is entirely within federal jurisdiction and is governed by the *Divorce Act*, which details the specific process for the dissolution of a marriage. Despite divorce being a federal matter, much of the fall-out from divorce lands in the provincial realm (e.g., the division of marital assets, etc.). Related topics: CHILDREN AND THE LAW, FAMILY LAW.

DIVORCE

Branche du droit de la FAMILLE, le divorce traite des moyens légaux de mettre fin au mariage. C'est un exemple, avec la FAILLITE, de droit privé de compétence fédérale. Cette loi pose le problème de l'interrelation avec le *Code civil du Québec*.

FISHER, GINETTE, AND LEANNE NOTENBOOM	*Canadian Family Law Guide*	CCH Cdn (LL)
SÉNÉCAL, JEAN-PIERRE	« Le divorce » dans *Droit de la famille québécois*	CCH (FM)
PAYNE, JULIEN, Q.C., AND MARILYN PAYNE	*Canadian Family Law*, 3d ed.	Irwin 2008
MACDONALD, JAMES C., AND ANN C. WILTON	*The 2007 Annotated* Divorce Act	Crswl 2006
PAYNE, JULIEN, Q.C., AND MARILYN PAYNE	*Child Support Guidelines in Canada, 2006*	Irwin 2006
PAYNE, JULIEN	*Payne on Divorce*, 4th ed.	Crswl 1996
MACDONALD, JAMES C., AND LEE K. FERRIER	*Canadian Divorce Law and Practice*	Crswl 1992
LABONTÉ, CHRISTIAN	« Le droit familial » dans *Personnes, famille et successions*	Y Blais 1995
HAINSWORTH, TERRY W.	Divorce Act *Manual*	CLB 1994

37·

EDUCATION LAW

This is an important, ever-growing area of the law that deals primarily with schooling. It is a matter of almost exclusive provincial jurisdiction although *Charter* issues sometimes enter this sphere (e.g., religious practices in public schools). Related topics: CHILDREN AND THE LAW, EMPLOYMENT LAW, HUMAN RIGHTS AND THE *CHARTER OF RIGHTS AND FREEDOMS*, INTELLECTUAL PROPERTY LAW, LABOUR LAW, OCCUPIER'S LIABILITY, TAXATION.

SCOLAIRE (DROIT)

Sous-ensemble du droit ADMINISTRATIF et analogue au droit MUNICIPAL bien que plus limité dans son domaine de compétence, le droit scolaire connaît de nombreux nouveaux développements dans le contexte des *CHARTES DES DROITS*, de l'ACCÈS À L'INFORMATION et de la PROPRIÉTÉ INTELLECTUELLE.

FARADAY, FAY	*Ontario Education Legislation, 2006-07*	CLB 2007
MILNE, CHERYL, AND MARTHA MACKINNON	*Education Statutes & Regulations of Ontario, 2007*	LN/B 2007
BROWN, ANTHONY F.	*Legal Handbook for Educators*, 5th ed.	Crswl 2004
BROWN, ANTHONY F., AND JUSTICE MARVIN A. ZUKER	*Education Law*, 3d ed.	Crswl 2002
GARANT, PATRICE	*Droit scolaire*	Y Blais 1992
MACKAY, A. WAYNE	*Education Law in Canada*	EM 1984

38.

EMPLOYMENT LAW

This topic relates to the employment of non-unionized workers (while Labour Law deals with unionized staff). This area is provincial in scope by way of the various provincial Employment Standards codes. Related topics: HUMAN RESOURCES LAW, LABOUR LAW.

TRAVAIL

C'est le domaine du droit dans lequel il se publie le plus de travaux, si l'on tient compte de la production des auteurs de relations industrielles. Le problème consiste plutôt à sélectionner l'ouvrage pertinent. Rappelons que le contrat individuel de travail est l'un des contrats nommés prévus au *Code civil*. L'arbitrage (travail) des griefs et différends fait l'objet d'une rubrique distincte de même que le sous-domaine de la SANTÉ ET SÉCURITÉ AU TRAVAIL.

Ball, Stacey R.	*Canadian Employment Law*	CLB (LL)
Barnacle, Peter, and Roderick Wood	*Employment Law in Canada*, 4th ed.	LN/B (LL)
Knight, James G., Lisa S. Goodfellow, and Carman J. Overholt	*Employment Litigation Manual*	LN/B (LL)
Mason, Rita	*Canadian Employment Law Guide*	CCH Cdn (LL)
Sproat, Justice John R.	*Employment Law Manual: Wrongful Dismissal, Human Rights and Employment Standards*	Crswl (LL)
England, Geoffrey	*Individual Employment Law*, 2d ed.	Irwin 2008
Morin, Fernand	*Fragments sur l'essentiel du droit de l'emploi*	W & LaF 2007
Morin, Fernand	*Le droit de l'emploi au Québec*, 3e éd.	W & LaF 2006

39.

ENERGY & NATURAL RESOURCES LAW

Given the significance of energy production to the economies of a number of provinces (e.g., oil and natural gas in Alberta, Saskatchewan, and the Atlantic provinces and hydro-electricity in Manitoba and Québec), and Canada's historic reputation as an exporter of natural resources, it is little wonder that this is becoming a very important area of the law throughout the country. It is an area of mixed jurisdictions and is heavily regulated at both the provincial and federal levels. Related topics: COMMERCIAL LAW, ENVIRONMENTAL LAW, EXPROPRIATION, *NAFTA (NORTH AMERICAN FREE TRADE AGREEMENT)*, NUISANCE, TAXATION, TRANSPORTATION LAW.

RESSOURCES NATURELLES

Vaste sous-ensemble du droit ADMINISTRATIF, le domaine public concerne le domaine de l'État en général et sa réglementation (par ex. terres dites « de la Couronne »). Plus particulièrement, on visera ici les questions relatives aux forêts, aux mines et aux pêches. Le partage des compétences en ce domaine a été légèrement modifié avec la *Loi constitutionnelle de 1982*. Les pêcheries, elles, demeurent de compétence fédérale.

Bennett Jones (law firm), and Nigel Bankes, eds.	*Canadian Oil & Gas*, 2d ed.	LN/B (LL)
Brown, David M.	*Energy Regulation in Ontario*	CLB (LL)
Canadian Institute of Resources Law	*Canada Energy Law Service* [Alta and federal]	Crswl (LL)
Carr, Brian R.	*Canadian Resource Taxation*	Crswl (LL)
Mancell, Gary E., Brian D. Gilfillan, and A.J. Davis	*Davis & Company's British Columbia Forestry Law: An Annotated Guide*	CLB (LL)
Barreau du Québec	*Développements récents en droit de l'énergie*	Y Blais 2007

♦ ENTERPRISE ou SERVICE (CONTRAT) voir CONTRACTS

ENTERTAINMENT & SPORTS LAW

An increasingly common area of practice, especially in the country's major centres, entertainment and sports law is particularly concerned with the law as it relates to artistic performers and athletes. Much of the research and practice in this topic is related to contracts, but there are other areas of activity as well, such as copyright, intellectual property, and negligence (e.g., sports injuries) *inter alia*. Most issues within this topic are rooted in jurisprudence. Related topics: AGENCY, COMMERCIAL LAW, LAW, CONTRACTS, COPYRIGHT, INTELLECTUAL PROPERTY LAW, NEGLIGENCE.

CULTURE ET DIVERTISSEMENT

La culture. Ce domaine couvre principalement les activités de création, de production, de diffusion, de commercialisation et de conservation reliées aux arts, aux lettres, aux industries culturelles, à la muséologie et au patrimoine. **Le divertissement.** Nouveau domaine du droit qui réunit sous l'angle des arts, de la culture et du divertissement les secteurs du droit des médias, de la propriété intellectuelle et des contrats. Voir aussi : AUTEUR (DROIT) ; COMMUNICATIONS (DROIT DES) ; CONTRATS ; PROPRIÉTÉ INTELLECTEULLE ; RESPONSABILITÉ CIVILE.

BARREAU DU QUÉBEC	*Développements récents en droit du divertissement*	Y Blais (LL)
DUARTE, TONY	*Canadian Film and Television Business and Legal Practice*	CLB (LL)
KING, JACQUELINE L.	*Entertainment Law in Canada*	LN/B (LL)
BARNES, JOHN	"Sports" in vol. 31, title 135.1 of the *Canadian Encyclopedic Digest* (Ontario) and vol. 32, title 136.1 of the *Canadian Encyclopedic Digest* (Western)	Crswl 2006
SANDERSON, PAUL E.	*Musicians and the Law in Canada*, 3d ed.	Crswl 2000
BARNES, JOHN	*Sports and the Law in Canada*, 3d ed.	LN/B 1996

41.

ENVIRONMENTAL LAW

This large area of the law deals with the protection of the natural environment from certain industrial and commercial activities, largely through statutory and regulatory enactments. There is a significant federal component by way of the *Canadian Environmental Protection Act, 1999* and its accompanying regulations, but there is also provincial legislation of relevance to the topic. Related topics: ADMINISTRATIVE LAW, CLASS ACTIONS, CRIMINAL LAW, ENERGY & NATURAL RESOURCES LAW, NEGLIGENCE, NUISANCE, REAL PROPERTY, TORTS.

ENVIRONNEMENT

Ce droit a pris un essor considérable et intéresse par son caractère souvent novateur. Nouveau domaine englobant et carrefour en même temps, l'environnement relève de façon duale du fédéral et des provinces et, là aussi, le contentieux CONSTITUTIONNEL surgit. La réglementation environnementale, proprement dite, est très développée et complexe ; elle empiète souvent sur les dimensions agricoles (AGRICULTURE ET CULTURE HYDROPONIQUE) ou d'aménagement et urbanisme ; elle pose ses limites au droit de propriété (BIENS ET PROPRIÉTÉ). Autour de ce noyau se développent, en amont, la prévention par les études d'impact (voir : ADMINISTRATIF (DROIT)) et, en aval, la punition par le droit pénal de l'environnement. L'apport des experts extérieurs au droit est important et, comme en BIOÉTHIQUE, de nombreux aspects relèvent d'autres disciplines (biologie animale ou végétale, génie minier ou forestier, hydraulique, etc.). Il touche tous les secteurs d'activités (transports, construction, habitation, production énergétique), ainsi que le patrimoine tant naturel que culturel (protection de la nature, des espèces, transport des déchets, sites classés, contaminants, biotechnologies, etc.).

BERGER, STANLEY D.	*The Prosecution and Defence of Environmental Offences*	CLB (LL)
LUCAS, ALASTAIR R., AND ROGER COTTON, eds.	*Canadian Environmental Law*, 2d ed.	LN/B (LL)
BENIDICKSON, JAMIE	*Environmental Law*, 3d ed.	Irwin 2009
ARBOUR, J.-MAURICE ET SOPHIE LAVALLÉE	*Droit international de l'environnement*	Y Blais 2007
MEUNIER, PIERRE B.	*Droit québécois de l'environnement*	Y Blais 2006
HUGHES, ELAINE L., ALASTAIR R. LUCAS, AND WILLIAM A. TILLEMAN	*Environmental Law and Policy*, 3d ed.	EM 2003
HALLEY, PAULE	*Le droit pénal de l'environnement : l'interdiction de polluer*	Y Blais 2001
PARDY, BRUCE	*Environmental Law: A Guide to Concepts*	LN/B 1996

EVIDENCE (CIVIL)

Evidence is the means by which an allegation of fact is substantiated at a judicial proceeding. It can be documentary, exhibitory, or oral. There are numerous rules surrounding the submission of evidence, making it a particularly complicated and actively researched area of the law. It is both federal and provincial in jurisdiction by way of the *Canada Evidence Act*, numerous provincial evidence acts, the rules of court for the various courts of the country, and evidentiary rules articulated in a variety of individual statutes. This topic lists works that deal primarily or exclusively with evidence in the context of a civil proceeding. Related topics: CIVIL PROCEDURE and EVIDENCE (CRIMINAL).

PREUVE CIVILE

Domaine principal du droit civil. Les règles sont les mêmes en civil et en commercial. La réforme a aussi prévu des règles pour la preuve informatique.

CUDMORE, GORDON	*Civil Evidence Handbook*	Crswl (LL)
ANDERSON, GLENN R.	*Expert Evidence*	LN/B 2005
PACIOCCO, DAVID, AND LEE STUESSER	*The Law of Evidence*, 5th ed.	Irwin 2008
DUCHARME, LÉO	*Précis de la prevue*, 6e éd.	W & LaF 2005
ROYER, JEAN-CLAUDE	*La preuve civile*, 3e éd.	Y Blais 2003
FRIEMAN, MARK J., AND MARK L. BERENBLUT	*The Litigator's Guide to Expert Witnesses*	CLB 1997
SCHIFF, STANLEY	*Evidence in the Litigation Process*	Crswl 1993
SOPINKA, JOHN, AND SIDNEY N. LEDERMAN	*The Law of Evidence in Civil Cases*	LN/B 1974

43.

EVIDENCE (CRIMINAL)

Evidence is the means by which an allegation of fact is substantiated at a judicial proceeding. It can be documentary, exhibitory, or oral. There are numerous rules surrounding the submission of evidence, making it a particularly complicated and actively researched area of the law. It is both federal and provincial in jurisdiction by way of the *Canada Evidence Act*, numerous provincial evidence acts, the rules of court for the various courts of the country, and evidentiary rules articulated in a variety of individual statutes. This section lists titles that deal exclusively or primarily with the law of evidence as it relates to criminal cases. Related topics: CRIMINAL LAW, CRIMINAL PROCEDURE, EVIDENCE (CIVIL).

PREUVE PÉNALE

Branche importante du droit CRIMINEL et du droit pénal. On applique essentiellement les mêmes règles dans les deux cas, sauf quant au degré de preuve requise. Le domaine statutaire provincial ne dispose pas de législation particulière à cet effet, il faut s'en remettre au droit statutaire fédéral.

HILL, JUSTICE CASEY *et al.*	*McWilliams' Canadian Criminal Evidence,* 4th ed.	CLB (LL)
PACIOCCO, DAVID, AND LEE STUESSER	*The Law of Evidence,* 5th ed.	Irwin 2008
BELIVEAU, PIERRE ET MARTIN VAUCLAIR	*Traité général de preuve et de procédure pénales,* 15e éd.	Thémis 2008
STEWART, HAMISH *et al.,* eds.	*Evidence: A Canadian Casebook,* 2d ed.	EM 2006
DELISLE, RON, DON STUART, AND DAVID M. TANOVICH	*Evidence: Principles and Problems,* 7th ed.	Crswl 2004
SOPINKA, JUSTICE JOHN, AND JUSTICE SIDNEY N. LEDERMAN	*The Law of Evidence in Canada,* 2d ed.	LN/B 2004
GOLD, ALAN D.	*Expert Evidence in Criminal Law: The Scientific Approach,* 2d ed.	Irwin 2009
PATENAUDE, PIERRE	*L'expertise en preuve pénale : les sciences et techniques modernes d'enquête, de surveillance et d'identification*	Y Blais 2003

44.

EXPROPRIATION

In normal circumstances, the state retains the right to purchase needed property regardless of the intentions of the property owner. This right is also known as "eminent domain." The only limit on the government's power is that it must pay a fair price for the expropriated property and this is normally the litigated issue in cases of expropriation. There is a federal *Expropriation Act* and numerous provincial counterparts. Related topics: MUNICIPAL LAW, REAL PROPERTY.

EXPROPRIATION

Le droit de l'expropriation réunit côte à côte l'intervention de l'État (ADMINISTRATIF (DROIT)) et un particulier avec ses BIENS ET PROPRIÉTÉ. Les opérations d'expropriation se situent souvent dans une perspective d'aménagement et urbanisme.

COATES, JOHN A., AND STEPHEN F. WAQUÉ	*New Law of Expropriation*	Crswl (LL)
MAKUCH, STANLEY M., NEIL CRAIK, AND SIGNE B. LEISK	*Canadian Municipal and Planning Law*, 2d ed.	Crswl 2004
LLOYD, SUSAN, AND ELIZABETH PORTMAN	"Expropriation" in vol. 12, title 60 of the *Canadian Encyclopedic Digest* (Ontario) and vol. 13, title 61 of the *Canadian Encyclopedic Digest* (Western)	Crswl 1998
TODD, ERIC C.E.	*The Law of Expropriation and Compensation in Canada*, 2d ed.	Crswl 1992
BOYD, KENNETH J.	*Expropriation in Canada: A Practitioner's Guide*	CLB 1988
LAJOIE, ANDRÉE	*Expropriation et fédéralisme au Canada*	Presses de l'Université de Montréal 1972

♦ FAILLITE ET INSOLVABILITÉ voir BANKRUPTCY & INSOLVENCY

45.

FAMILY LAW

This is an immense area of the law that crosses a large number of subtopics. It is also an area of very active litigation, mediation, and research. Its major subtopics include marriage, divorce, children, child custody, and division of family assets, *inter alia*. Some of these areas are federal in scope, such as divorce, by way of the *Divorce Act*, and some aspects of marriage, by way of the *Marriage (Prohibited Degrees) Act*, but most facets of this area remain provincial in scope. Related topics: ADOPTION, CHILDREN AND THE LAW, DIVORCE, TAXATION.

FAMILLE

Branche principale du droit civil, le droit de la famille inclut les questions de donation, du patrimoine familial et de son partage en cas de DIVORCE et de séparation. Certains auteurs y ajoutent la personne.

CHRISTOPHER, T. CATHERINE	*The Law of Domestic Conflict in Canada*	Crswl (LL)
FISHER, GINETTE, AND LEANNE NOTENBOOM	*Canadian Family Law Guide*	CCH Cdn (LL)
HOLLAND, WINIFRED, AND BARBRO STALBACKER-POUNTNEY	*Cohabitation: The Law in Canada*	Crswl (LL)
MCLEOD, JAMES G.	*Matrimonial Property Law in Canada*	Crswl (LL)
PAYNE, JULIEN D., Q.C., AND MARILYN PAYNE	*Canadian Family Law*, 3d ed.	Irwin 2008
PINEAU, JEAN	*La famille*	Thémis 2006
CASTELLI, MIREILLE D.	*Le droit de la famille au Québec*	Université Laval 2005
TÉTRAULT, MICHEL	*Droit de la famille*	Y Blais 2005
MOSSMAN, MARY JANE	*Families and the Law in Canada: Cases and Commentary*	EM 2004
FODDEN, SIMON	*Family Law*	Irwin 1999

- FIDUCIE voir TRUSTS
- FISCALITÉ voir TAXATION

46.

FRANCHISING LAW

A franchise is essentially a privilege that is sold, licensed, or granted from one party to another. In commerce, this normally means the right granted from the holder of a trade-mark to another to trade under that name or to sell its products. In the normal course of events, the franchisee pays the franchisor money in order to sell the franchisor's products and in return the franchisor undertakes to promote the product. A large proportion of the Canadian retail sector operates in this manner. Related topics: AGENCY, COMMERCIAL LAW, CONTRACTS, SALE OF GOODS.

FRANCHISE

Le CONTRAT de franchise est un moyen de financement et de développement d'une entreprise ; il constitue un élément important du droit des AFFAIRES. En raison de l'implication des multinationales, le contrat de franchise recèle souvent une dimension de droit INTERNATIONAL PRIVÉ et s'insère, à l'occasion, dans une dynamique de contrats internationaux.

GAGNON, JEAN H.	La franchise au Québec	W & LaF (FM)
LEVITT, EDWARD N.	Canadian Franchise Legislation	LN/B (LL)
WHITE, JERRY, AND FRANK ZAID	Canadian Franchise Guide	Crswl (LL)
SNELL, PETER, AND LARRY WEINBERG, eds.	Fundamentals of Franchising, Canada	American Bar Association Forum on Franchising 2005
SO, DANIEL F.	Canadian Franchise Law Handbook	LN/B 2005
ZAID, FRANK	Franchise Law	Irwin 2005
DENAULT, PHILIPPE ET LORETTE COLTON	Le franchisage	Y Blais 1993
BOURRET, JEAN J. et al.	Le franchisage : l'entrepreneuriat encadré	Québec, ministère de l'Industrie 1992
CHOQUETTE, JEAN L.	Initiation à la franchise : réussir et vivre son projet : pour les futurs franchisés	Agence d'ARC 1991
MATHIEU, PAUL-ANDRÉ	La nature juridique du contrat de franchise	Y Blais 1989

47.

GAMING & LOTTERIES

As various governments in Canada are becoming increasingly dependant upon the revenue generated from lottery schemes and provincially established and regulated casinos, this area of the law is rapidly becoming more developed. It involves all facets of gambling, horse and dog racing, lotteries, casinos, and charitable gaming. The criminal aspects of gambling are federal in scope, by way of the *Criminal Code*, but the licensing of gaming and lotteries is a provincial matter. However, there is some constitutional confusion with regard to gaming on aboriginal reserves, which are normally deemed to be federal in jurisdiction. Related topics: ABORIGINAL LAW, CHARITIES & CHARITABLE CORPORATIONS, CONSTITUTIONAL LAW, CRIMINAL LAW.

JEUX ET LOTERIES

Le jeu et le pari sont prévus au *Code civil* comme contrat nommé. La réglementation des loteries relève du droit ADMINISTRATIF et les loteries illégales du droit CRIMINEL.

CASTEL, JACQUELINE RUTH	*Gaming Control Law in Ontario*	CLB (LL)
BELANGER, YALE DERON	*Gambling with the Future: The Evolution of Aboriginal Gambling in Canada*	Purich Publishing 2006
BOURGEOIS, DONALD J.	*The Law of Charitable and Casino Gaming*	LN/B 1999
LEECH, PATRICK	"Gaming" in vol. 14, title 67 of the *Canadian Encyclopedic Digest* (Ontario) and vol. 15, title 69 of the *Canadian Encyclopedic Digest* (Western)	Crswl 1998
SMITH, COLIN M., AND STEPHEN P. MONCKOM	*Law of Betting Gaming and Lotteries* (U.K.)	LN/B 1987

48.

HEALTH LAW

The term "Health Law" is being used to incorporate a vast number of disparate topics generally related to the various health professions: medicine, nursing, and dentistry, etc. Most often the nexus between these professions and law comes about by way of malpractice/negligence litigation, but this is not exclusively the case. For the most part, this is an area that is provincial in scope in that the provinces grant the various professional groups, by way of delegated powers, the authority to establish the criteria for membership in their professions and the rights of discipline and dismissal. They also establish professional standards and are normally the first to judge professional competence of their members. Related topics: ADMINISTRATIVE LAW, BIOETHICS, NEGLIGENCE, OCCUPATIONAL HEALTH & SAFETY, PROFESSIONAL RESPONSIBILITY, TORTS.

SANTÉ – MÉDECINE

Droit de la santé et droit médical, les deux expressions ont cours même si elles ne couvrent pas toujours la même réalité. Certains aspects du droit de la santé qui touchent aux régimes sociaux (par ex. assurance-hospitalisation) relèvent en réalité de la sécurité sociale. Les règles de la RESPONSABILITÉ CIVILE sont généralement appliquées. Voir aussi : RESPONSABILITÉ PROFESSIONNELLE ; BIOÉTHIQUE ; DROITS DE LA PERSONNE ET *CHARTE CANADIENNE DES DROITS ET LIBERTÉS*.

QUÉBEC	*Droit de la santé : lois et règlements annotés*	Y Blais (FM)
ROZOVSKY, LORNE ELKIN	*Canadian Law of Consent to Treatment*, 3d ed.	LN/B (LL)
PHILIPS-NOOTENS, SUZANNE *et al.*	*Éléments de responsabilité civile médicale*, 3e éd.	Y Blais 2007
BLOOM, HY, AND RICHARD D. SCHNEIDER	*Mental Disorder and the Law: A Primer for Legal and Mental Health Professionals*	Irwin 2006
BAILEY, TRACEY M., TIMOTHY A. CAULFIELD, AND NOLA M. RIES, eds.	*Public Health Law and Policy in Canada*	LN/B 2005
DUPLESSIS, YVON	*L'accès à l'information et la protection des renseignements personnels : santé et services sociaux*	CCH 2005
BARAKETT, RAYMOND	*Précis annoté de la Loi sur les services de santé et les services sociaux*, 4e éd.	Y Blais 2004
DOWNIE, JOCELYN, KAREN McEWEN, AND WILLIAM MacINNIS	*Dental Law in Canada*	LN/B 2004
SNEIDERMAN, BARNEY, PHILIP H. OSBORNE, AND JOHN C. IRVINE	*Canadian Medical Law: An Introduction for Physicians, Nurses, and Other Health Care Professionals*, 3d ed.	Crswl 2003
ROBERTSON, GERALD B., AND ELLEN I. PICARD	*Legal Liability of Doctors and Hospitals*, 3d ed.	Crswl 1996

49.

HUMAN RESOURCES LAW

In contrast with Employment and Labour law, which deal with the statutes that detail the rules surrounding the employment, discipline, and dismissal of employees, Human Resources law is a much broader and varied topic. It deals with a wide range of employment related matters such as harassment in the workplace, duties to accommodate, rights of employee privacy, etc. Most matters within this topic will be provincial in scope, and some grounded in caselaw. Related topics: EMPLOYMENT LAW, HUMAN RIGHTS AND THE *CHARTER OF RIGHTS AND FREEDOMS*, LABOUR LAW, OCCUPATIONAL HEALTH & SAFETY, PENSIONS, PRIVACY LAW & ACCESS TO INFORMATION, WORKERS' COMPENSATION.

RESSOURCES HUMAINES

Sous-ensemble du droit du TRAVAIL, ce domaine concerne de nombreux aspects de l'emploi autres que la discipline et le congédiement. Mentionnons : le harcèlement, l'accommodement, la vie privée, etc. Voir aussi : SANTÉ ET SÉCURITÉ AU TRAVAIL.

MOLE, ELLEN E., AND JOHN A. BOLLAND	*Best Practices: Employment Policies that Work*	Crswl (LL)
MOSER, CINDY	*Human Resources Management in Canada*	Crswl (LL)
THOMAS, M. MICHAEL, AND SUSAN M. SINGH	*Canadian Benefits Administration Manual*	Crswl (LL)
BRIÈRE, JEAN-YVES	*Questions et réponses en gestion des ressources humaines, 3e éd.*	CCH 2007
AGGARWAL, ARJUN, AND MADHU GUPTA	*Sexual Harassment: A Guide for Understanding and Prevention, 2d ed.*	LN/B 2006
BOURGAULT, JULIE	*Le harcèlement psychologique au travail : les nouvelles dispositions de la Loi sur les normes et leur intégration dans le régime légal préexistant*	W & LaF 2006
CANTIN, ISABELLE	*Politiques contre le harcèlement au travail et réflexions sur le harcèlement psychologique, 2e éd.*	Y Blais 2006
EDWARDS, J.J.	*Human Resources Guide to Workplace Privacy*	Aurora Professional Press 2003
BRUNELLE, CHRISTIAN	*Discrimination et obligation d'accommodement en milieu de travail syndiqué*	Y Blais 2001

50.

HUMAN RIGHTS AND THE *CHARTER OF RIGHTS AND FREEDOMS*

The topic of Human Rights takes into consideration all matters related to discriminatory interactions between private citizens, individuals, and the state. Human Rights statutes guarantee citizens protections from discrimination based on attributes such as race, religion, gender, etc., in a variety of settings (e.g., employment, housing). A specific and fundamental subset of Human Rights is the *Charter of Rights and Freedoms*, which is a component part of the federal *Consitution Act, 1982*. Since its passage, accompanied by the repatriation from the U.K. of the Canadian Constitution by the government of Pierre Elliot Trudeau, the *Charter* has become the principal guarantor of human and civil rights within the country. It has also had the effect of expanding other rights (e.g., language rights) and has reversed the balance of power between the judiciary and Parliament by making Parliament's (and the provincial legislatures') enactments subject to review by the courts as to their compliance with the *Charter*. Prior to the enactment of the *Charter*, the concept of Parliamentary supremacy severely limited the courts' ability to scrutinize federal legislation. The *Charter* is federal and applies to the country as a whole, but has an impact on many areas of provincial jurisdiction. It is critical to remember, however, that the *Charter*'s reach is limited exclusively to state action (broadly defined). Related topics: ABORIGINAL LAW, CONSTITUTIONAL LAW, CRIMINAL LAW, CRIMINAL PROCEDURE, YOUNG OFFENDERS.

DROITS DE LA PERSONNE ET *CHARTE CANADIENNE DES DROITS ET LIBERTÉS*

Ce domaine a connu une telle effervescence depuis 1976 au Québec et depuis 1982 au fédéral que le problème documentaire réside dans la pléthore plutôt que dans la rareté. La documentation est immense, éparse et d'origine multiple. Pour mémoire, rappelons seulement qu'il existe non seulement plusieurs chartes, mais de nombreuses lois statutaires complémentaires aux champs d'application distincts; rappelons ensuite que ces chartes ont été plaidées universellement et constamment : il en résulte des recoupements entre la charte et un domaine donné, parfois restreint (par ex. l'alcootest). L'apport étranger, notamment européen et américain, n'est pas à négliger dans ce domaine et, là encore, les outils abondent. La problématique des chartes se place dans l'horizon plus vaste du droit CONSTITUTIONNEL.

CASEY, JAMES T., ed.	*Remedies In Labour, Employment, and Human Rights Law*	Crswl (LL)
LASKIN, JOHN B., EDWARD L. GREENSPAN, Q.C., AND MELANIE DUNN	*Canadian Charter of Rights Annotated*	CLB (LL)
PENTNEY, WILLIAM	*Discrimination and the Law*	Crswl (LL)
ROACH, KENT	*Constitutional Remedies in Canada*	CLB (LL)

ZINN, RUSSEL W.	*The Law of Human Rights in Canada: Practice and Procedure*	CLB (LL)
RAY-ELLIS, SOMA	"Discrimination and Human Rights," a vol. of *Halsbury's Laws of Canada*, 1st ed.	LN/B 2008
LEMONDE, LUCIE *et al.*	*Les 25 ans de la* Charte canadienne des droits et libertés	Y Blais 2007
BEAUDOIN, GÉRALD-A., AND ERROL MENDES	Canadian Charter of Rights & Freedoms, 3d ed.	LN/B 2005
SHARPE, ROBERT J., KATHERINE E. SWINTON, AND KENT ROACH	*The* Charter of Rights and Freedoms, 3d ed.	Irwin 2005
STUART, DON	Charter *Justice in Canadian Criminal Law,* 4th ed.	Crswl 2005
MAGNET, JOSEPH E., ed.	*The* Canadian Charter of Rights and Freedoms: *Reflections on the* Charter *After Twenty Years*	LN/B 2003
BRUNELLE, CHRISTIAN	« Les droits et libertés fondamentaux » dans *Droit publique et administratif*	Y Blais 1995
TARNOPOLSKY, WALTER, JOYCE WHITMAN, AND MONIQUE OUELLETTE, eds.	*Discrimination in the Law and the Administration of Justice*	Thémis 1993

51.

IMMIGRATION & CITIZENSHIP

Since the passage and commencement, in 1946 and 1947 respectively, of the federal *Canadian Citizenship Act* (now simply the *Citizenship Act*), the issue of Canadian citizenship and its acquisition has been strictly and unequivocally a matter of federal jurisdiction. Immigration to Canada is governed by the *Immigration & Protection of Refugees Act*. There are, however, arrangements made between the federal government and various provincial governments (all but Ontario) by which immigrants will be directed to certain provinces according to the articulated list of desired skills and training set out by the specific province. A significant subset of this topic is that related to refugees and those seeking asylum in Canada. Related topic: REFUGEES.

IMMIGRATION

Branche du droit public de compétence fédérale. On évitera de la confondre avec la citoyenneté, une question étudiée en droit CONSTITUTIONNEL et tangentiellement en DROITS DE LA PERSONNE ET *CHARTE CANADIENNE DES DROITS ET LIBERTÉS*. L'immigration concerne le droit d'entrer au Canada pour y demeurer ou y séjourner, parfois en vue d'obtenir la citoyenneté. Il s'agit de droit ADMINISTRATIF, la plupart du temps, bien que certaines dimensions relèvent des chartes des droits, voir du droit CRIMINEL. Les mêmes autorités administratives disposent souvent des questions des RÉFUGIÉS. Les dimensions de droit INTERNATIONAL PUBLIC sont présentes à l'horizon.

WALDMAN, LORNE	*Immigration Law and Practice*, 2d ed.	LN/B (LL)
JONES, MARTIN, AND SASHA BAGLAY	*Refugee Law*	Irwin 2007
WALDMAN, LORNE	*Canadian Immigration and Refugee Law Practice*, 2007 ed.	LN/B 2007
CARASCO, EMILY *et al.*	*Immigration and Refugee Law: Cases, Materials, and Commentary*	EM 2006
CHAMBRES DE COMMERCE FRANÇAISE AU CANADA *et al.*	*Guide de l'immigration au Québec: histoire, démarches, budget, emploi, investissements: votre intégration pas à pas*	Néopol 2006
WALDMAN, LORNE	"Immigration and Citizenship," a vol. of *Halsbury's Laws of Canada*, 1st ed.	LN/B 2006
BARREAU DU QUÉBEC	*Développements récents en droit de l'immigration*	Y Blais 1998
GALLOWAY, DONALD	*Immigration Law*	Irwin 1997
TRISTER, BENJAMIN J., AND NAN BEREZOWSKI	*Citizenship*	Crswl 1996

- INTERNATIONAL PRIVÉ (DROIT) voir PRIVATE INTERNATIONAL LAW
- INTERNATIONAL PUBLIC (DROIT) voir PUBLIC INTERNATIONAL LAW

INFORMATION TECHNOLOGY LAW

This is a rapidly expanding subject in Canadian law. Generally speaking, it relates to all manner of legal implications associated with information technology (computers, PDAs, blackberries, IPODs, *inter alia*). Its major subtopics include computer crime, e-commerce, circuit board and database design and protection, domain names, software licensing, etc. There are also a number of privacy and intellectual property issues at play in this topic (primarily copyright and trade-mark). The intellectual property matters are essentially federal in scope, while most other issues fall under provincial jurisdiction. There is an ever growing body of jurisprudence in this area, as well. Related topics: COMMERCIAL LAW, COPYRIGHT LAW, CRIMINAL LAW, INTELLECTUAL PROPERTY LAW, PRIVACY LAW & ACCESS TO INFORMATION, TRADE-MARKS.

TECHNOLOGIES DE L'INFORMATION (DROIT DES)

Il ne s'agit évidemment pas d'une réalité juridique, mais l'importance actuelle et croissante du plus vaste « réseau de réseaux » justifie qu'on en fasse mention. Trois aspects complémentaires méritent une mention : (i) l'introduction générale à Internet et les moyens techniques de s'y brancher ; (ii) les problèmes juridiques posés par Internet et qui recoupent les domaines du droit : CRIMINEL (DROIT) ; PROPRIÉTÉ INTELLECTUELLE ; ACCÈS À L'INFORMATION ; COMMUNICATIONS (DROIT DES) ; (iii) la recherche d'informations juridiques au moyen de Internet, un volet complémentaire à une démarche de RECHERCHE DOCUMENTAIRE.

SOOKMAN, BARRY B.	*Sookman: Computer, Internet, and Electronic Commerce Law*	Crswl (LL)
ASSOCIATION DU JEUNE BARREAU DE MONTRÉAL	*Legal TI : droit et technologies de l'information : devenir aujourd'hui, l'avocat de demain*	Y Blais 2007
ABE, LISA K., MARIE-HÉLÈNE CONSTANTIN, AND SUNNY HANDA	*Web Law: Agreements, Guidelines and Use Policies*	LN/B 2005
DETURBIDE, MICHAEL, AND TERESA SCASSA	*Electronic Commerce and Internet Law in Canada*	CCH Cdn 2004
TAKACH, GEORGE	*Computer Law*, 2d ed.	Irwin 2003
GAHTAN, ALAN M., MARTIN P.J. KRATZ, AND J. FRASER MANN	*Internet Law: A Practical Guide for Legal and Business Professionals*	Crswl 1998
HUTCHISON, SCOTT C., AND ROBERT W. DAVIS	*Computer Crime in Canada*	Crswl 1997

53.

INSURANCE LAW

Often treated as a particular subset of contract law, the law of insurance is a large and particularly complex area of Canadian law. Dealing with all types of insurance (health, liability, life, marine, motor vehicle, property, etc.) it is predominantly within the sphere of the provinces and is also greatly informed by a large body of jurisprudence. There are, however, two significant federal statutes that regulate insurers insofar as they function as financial institutions: The *Insurance Companies Act* and the *Office of the Superintendant of Financial Institutions Act*. Related topics: BANKING LAW, COMMERCIAL LAW, CONTRACTS.

ASSURANCES

Mécanisme de règlement des différends très répandu en droit du TRAVAIL, l'arbitrage de griefs implique, en ce domaine, des règles utilisées en ARBITRAGE (CIVIL ET COMMERCIAL).

Brown, Craig, and Julio Menezes	*Insurance Law in Canada*	Crswl (LL)
Boivin, Denis	*Le droit des assurances dans les provinces de Common Law*	LN/B 2006
Brown, Craig	*Introduction to Canadian Insurance Law, 2d ed.*	LN/B 2006
Hilliker, Gordon	*Liability Insurance Law in Canada, 4th ed.*	LN/B 2006
Lluelles, Didier	*Précis des assurances terrestres, 4e éd.*	Thémis 2005
Boivin, Denis	*Insurance Law*	Irwin 2004
Norwood, David, and John P. Weir	*Norwood on Life Insurance Law in Canada, 3d ed.*	Crswl 2002

54.

INTELLECTUAL PROPERTY LAW

This is the law related to the protection of ideas and expression. Normally, this topic is divided into the following subtopics: copyright, industrial design, patents, and trade-marks. These specific areas are all subject to federal legislation, placing this area in the federal sphere. There are also biotechnology, information technology, and privacy aspects to the topic. This listing deals generally with intellectual property because the specific subtopics (other than industrial design) are dealt with individually elsewhere. Related topics: COPYRIGHT, INFORMATION TECHNOLOGY LAW, PATENTS, PRIVACY LAW & ACCESS TO INFORMATION, TRADE-MARKS.

PROPRIÉTÉ INTELLECTUELLE

Le droit de la propriété intellectuelle (PI) couvre sous l'angle de la propriété des droits, le vaste domaine des arts, de la culture et du divertissement. Du slogan publicitaire à la carte génétique, de la molécule oléophage au circuit informatique, rien n'échappe au nouveau droit de la propriété intellectuelle. Aux branches traditionnelles du domaine – DROIT D'AUTEUR, BREVETS, MARQUES DE COMMERCE et dessin industriel – s'ajoutent maintenant les questions relatives aux circuits informatiques, aux obtentions végétales et à la brevetabilité du vivant en général à l'exclusion des aspects humains, ces derniers relevant de la BIOÉTHIQUE.

UNIVERSITÉ MCGILL, FACULTÉ DE DROIT	*Nouvelles approches en propriété intellectuelle dans un monde transsystémique / Intellectual Property at the Edge: New Approaches to IP in a Transsystematic World*	Y Blais 2007
GENDREAU, YSOLDE, DIR.	*Propriété intellectuelle : entre l'art et l'argent*	Thémis 2006
GERVAIS, DANIEL J.	*Le droit de la propriété intellectuelle*	Crswl 2006
JUDGE, ELIZABETH F., AND DANIEL GERVAIS	*Intellectual Property: The Law in Canada*	Crswl 2005
FECENKO, MARK J.	*Biotechnology Law: Corporate-Commercial Practice*	LN/B 2002
HOWELL, ROBERT G., LINDA VINCENT, AND MICHAEL D. MANSON	*Intellectual Property Law: Cases and Materials*	EM 1999
VAVER, DAVID	*Intellectual Property Law: Copyright, Patents, Trade-Marks*	Irwin 1997
CORNISH, DIANE E.	*Licensing Intellectual Property*	Crswl 1995

INTERNATIONAL SALE OF GOODS

This topic is essentially concerned with business transactions in which goods are sold across international boundaries, either via import into Canada or export out of the country. It is ruled by a large, federal regulatory framework. Related topics: INTERNATIONAL TRADE LAW and *NAFTA (NORTH AMERICAN FREE TRADE AGREEMENT)*.

VENTE INTERNATIONALE

Important contrat nommé du droit COMMERCIAL INTERNATIONAL, la vente internationale est d'abord une vente ordinaire dont plusieurs modalités obéissent à une importante convention internationale, la convention dite « de Vienne » sur la vente internationale de marchandises.

GUILLEMARD, SYLVETTE	*Le droit international privé face au contrat de vente cyberspatial*	Y Blais 2006
FAWCETT, J.J.	*International Sale of Goods in the Conflict of Laws* (U.K. & U.S.)	OUP 2005
LEFEBVRE, GUY	*Les principes d'UNIDROIT et les contrats internationaux: aspects pratiques*	Thémis 2003
ENDERLEIN, FRITZ	*International Sales Law: United Nations Convention on Contracts for the International Sale of Goods* (U.S.)	Oceana 2002
INSTITUTE OF CONTINUING LEGAL EDUCATION	*Drafting Essentials: How to Internationalize Your Commercial Contracts*	Ontario Bar Association 2002
LAMAZEROLLES, EDDY	*Les apports de la Convention de Vienne au droit interne de la vente*	Université de Poitiers 2000
KLOTZ, JAMES M.	*International Sales Agreements: An Annotated Drafting and Negotiation Guide*	CLB 1997
MAGRAW, DANIEL BARSTOW, AND KATHERINE R. REED	*The Convention for the International Sale of Goods: A Handbook of Basic Materials*, 2d ed. (U.S.)	American Bar Association, Section of International Law and Practice 1990

INTERNATIONAL TRADE LAW

Given the increasing importance of international trade to Canada's economy, this is an area of expanding research and litigation. Dominated by the *NAFTA*, this area of law is subject to federal legislation and other international conventions and treaties, such as the *General Agreement on Tariffs & Trade* (*GATT*) and the *World Trade Organization Agreement* (*WTO*). Related topics: INTERNATIONAL SALE OF GOODS and *NAFTA*.

COMMERCIAL INTERNATIONAL (DROIT)

Très vaste domaine qui couvre les aspects juridiques des relations commerciales internationales (CONTRATS, ARBITRAGE (CIVIL ET COMMERCIAL)). Strictement parlant, s'agissant de relations de droit privé entre des particuliers qui font des affaires entre eux, le domaine devrait relever du droit INTERNATIONAL PRIVÉ. Deux raisons, toutefois, s'opposent à cette simplification. Premièrement, une bonne partie du DCI (Droit commercial international) repose dans des conventions internationales étatiques qui, comme telles, relèvent du droit INTERNATIONAL PUBLIC: le Canada y adhère et la convention s'applique. Deuxièmement, de nombreux aspects complémentaires appartenant au droit international économique (monnaie, systèmes de paiements, banques centrales, aide à l'investissement, protection de l'investissement étranger, etc.) touchent de près les activités commerciales. L'ARBITRAGE (CIVIL ET COMMERCIAL) fait l'objet d'une réglementation au *Code civil*.

NAVARRO, JEAN-LOUIS ET GUY LEFEBVRE	*L'acculturation en droit des affaires*	Thémis 2007
BACHAND, FRÉDÉRIC	*L'intervention du juge canadien avant et durant un arbitrage commercial international*	Y Blais 2005
FORTIN, PHILIPPE	*La pratique du commerce international*	CCH Cdn 2005
KOSAR, WILLIAM E.	*Cases and Materials: International Business & Trade Law as Applied and Interpreted in Canada*	Crswl 2005
INTERNATIONAL TRADE CENTRE	*Business Guide to Trade Remedies in Canada: Anti-Dumping, Countervailing, and Safeguards Legislation, Practices and Procedures*	United Nations 2003
LEFEBVRE, GUY	*Les principes d'UNIDROIT et les contrats internationaux: aspects pratiques*	Thémis 2003
JOHNSON, JON R.	*International Trade Law*	Irwin 1998
CASTEL, J.-G. et al.	*The Canadian Law and Practice of International Trade*, 2d ed.	EM 1997
PATERSON, ROBERT K., AND MARTINE M.N. BAND	*International Trade and Investment Law in Canada*, 2d ed.	Crswl 1995

57.

LABOUR LAW

This term refers to the law of employment as it relates to unionized workers (as opposed to employment law, which deals more generally with the subject and with non-unionized employees). It is an area of primarily provincial competence, by way of various provincial labour relations acts, however there is a significant piece of federal legislation, the *Canada Labour Code*, that governs any situations involving work being done for or by the federal government or its agencies. Related topic: EMPLOYMENT LAW.

TRAVAIL

Les principes généraux sont souvent commentés avec le droit provincial, mais de nombreux détails substantiels et procéduraux expliquent le traitement autonome de cet ensemble normatif qui vise les relations de travail de compétence fédérale (communication, fonction publique fédérale, ouvrages fédéraux, etc.).

ADAMS, GEORGE W., AND SANDRA ADAMS	*Canadian Labour Law*, 2d ed.	CLB (LL)
BROWN, DAVID M., AND DAVID M. BEATTY	*Canadian Labour Arbitration*, 4th ed.	CLB (LL)
GAGNON, ROBERT P. ET K.D. LANGLOIS	*Le droit du travail du Québec*, 6e éd.	Y Blais 2008
COUTU, MICHEL *et al.*	*Droit administratif du travail : tribunaux et organismes spécialisés du domaine du travail*	Y Blais 2007
HÉBERT, GÉRARD *et al.*	*La convention collective au Québec*	Gaëtan Morin 2007
MITCHNICK, MORTON, AND BRIAN ETHERINGTON	*Labour Arbitration in Canada*	Lancaster House 2006
MORIN, FERNAND	*Le droit de l'emploi au Québec*, 3e éd.	W & LaF 2006
VERGE, PIERRE	*Le droit du travail par ses sources*	Thémis 2006
LABOUR LAW CASEBOOK GROUP	*Labour and Employment Law: Cases, Materials, and Commentary*, 7th ed.	Irwin 2004
LE CORRE, CLAUDE	*La syndicalisation sous le Code du travail : avant, pendant et après, tout ce que l'employeur doit savoir*, 2e éd.	Y Blais 2004
CARTER, DONALD D. *et al.*	*Labour Law in Canada*, 5th ed.	LN/B 2002

58.

LANDLORD & TENANT

This topic, which deals with the rental of property, is normally confined to commercial tenancies while residential tenancies are normally treated separately. This list includes both. This is an area of exclusively provincial domain and there is legislation in each province dealing with commercial and residential tenancies. Related topic: HUMAN RIGHTS AND THE *CHARTER OF RIGHTS AND FREEDOMS*, REAL PROPERTY.

LOGEMENT LOCATIF (LOUAGE)

Sous-ensemble particulier du louage, le logement locatif mérite une rubrique à part en double raison du nombre de personnes impliquées et du fait qu'une partie de la réglementation provient du droit statutaire et, comme telle, relève du droit ADMINISTRATIF.

ALBERT, CAROL A., ROBERT G. DOUMANI, AND JOY OVERTVELD	*Ontario Residential Tenancies Law*	Crswl (LL)
BENTLEY, CHRISTOPHER A.W., JOHN MCNAIR, AND MAVIS J. BUTKUS	*Williams and Rhodes' Canadian Law of Landlord and Tenant*, 6th ed.	Crswl (LL)
OLSON, RICHARD	*A Commercial Tenancy Handbook*	Crswl (LL)
HABER, HARVEY M.	*Understanding the Commercial Agreement to Lease*, 2d ed.	CLB 2006
LAMONT, DONALD H.L., AND RICHARD FELDMAN	*Residential Tenancies*, 7th ed.	Crswl 2006
DESLAURIERS, JACQUES	*Vente, louage, contrat d'entreprise ou de service*	W & LaF 2005
LAMONTAGNE, DENYS-CLAUDE ET BERNARD LAROCHELLE	*Droit spécialisé des contrats*	Y Blais 1999

59.

LANGUAGE LAW

In a nation that is officially bilingual, language is naturally an area of frequent research and occasional litigation. Official bilingualism is only the case federally, via the *Official Languages Act* and in the province of New Brunswick (*Official Languages Act*). The official language of Québec is French, whereas it is English in the remaining eight provinces and three territories. Language rights are also articulated in the *Charter* and it is under the *Charter* that most language litigation arises. Related topics: CONSTITUTIONAL LAW, HUMAN RIGHTS AND THE *CHARTER OF RIGHTS AND FREEDOMS*.

LANGUE

Le Québec est une terre fertile pour la jurilinguistique. Ce domaine, aux confins inexplorés, regroupe les nombreuses interfaces entre le droit et la langue : législation linguistique proprement dite, bilinguisme, terminologie juridique, etc. Plusieurs aspects touchent aux DROITS DE LA PERSONNE ET *CHARTE CANADIENNE DES DROITS ET LIBERTÉS*). La plupart des ouvrages de droit CONSTITUTIONNEL abordent les questions linguistiques.

BRAËN, ANDRÉ, PIERRE FOUCHER, AND YVES LE BOUTHILLIER, eds.	*Languages, Constitutionalism, and Minorities*	LN/B 2006
CANADA	*Canada's Linguistic Duality: A Framework to Manage the* Official Languages Act	Government of Canada 2005
GÉMAR, JEAN-CLAUDE ET NICHOLAS KASIRER	*Jurilinguistique : entre langues et droits / Jurilinguistics: Between Law and Language*	Thémis 2005
BASTARACHE, MICHEL	*Les droits linguistiques au Canada*	Y Blais 2004
BASTARACHE, MICHEL	*Language Rights in Canada*, 2d ed.	Y Blais 2003
QUÉBEC	Charte de la langue française *et règlements d'application avec notes explicatives et jurisprudence*	Office de la langue française 2002
MAGNET, JOSEPH ELIOT	*Official Languages of Canada*	Y Blais 1995
FOUCHER, PIERRE	*Constitutional Rights of Official-Language Minorities in Canada*	Canadian Legal Information Centre 1985

60.

LEGAL ETHICS

In contrast to the perception of much of the public, law as a profession has, at its core, a body of ethical considerations and constantly seeks to balance interests and achieve fairness in process and result. As such, legal ethics are an important matter to all participants in the profession. They are expressed in a variety of ways: through academic writing, professional discussion, rules of court, and guidelines set out by the profession itself. Related topic: PROFESSIONAL RESPONSIBILITY.

DISCIPLINAIRE (DROIT)

Sous-ensemble du droit des professions, le droit disciplinaire mérite une mention autonome en raison de sa spécificité et de sa place intermédiaire entre le droit pénal et le droit de la RESPONSABILITÉ CIVILE. La discipline dans les milieux de travail relève du droit du TRAVAIL. La discipline dans la fonction publique est étudiée en droit ADMINISTRATIF.

MACNAIR, M. DEBORAH	*Conflict of Interest: Principles for the Legal Profession*	CLB (LL)
NOREAU, PIERRE	*La déontologie judiciaire appliqué*, 2e éd.	W & LaF 2008
MACKENZIE, GAVIN	*Lawyers and Ethics: Professional Responsibility and Discipline*, 4th ed.	Crswl 2006
TÉTRAULT, MICHEL	*Le litige familial, la déontologie et l'éthique*	Y Blais 2006
HUTCHISON, ALLAN C.	*Legal Ethics and Professional Responsibility*, 2d ed.	Irwin 2006
PROULX, HON. MICHEL, AND DAVID LAYTON	*Ethics and Canadian Criminal Law*	Irwin 2001
BARREAU DU QUÉBEC	*Développements récents en déontologie, droit professionnel et disciplinaire*	Y Blais 1998
BUCKINGHAM, DONALD E.	*Legal Ethics in Canada: Theory and Practice*	Harcourt Brace Canada 1996
CANADIAN BAR ASSOCIATION	*Code of Professional Conduct*	Canadian Bar Association 1987

61.

LEGAL PRACTICE

This listing deals with the legal profession as a business and includes titles aimed at assisting members of the profession in their role as barristers and solicitors. Related topics: LEGAL ETHICS, PROFESSIONAL RESPONSIBILITY.

PRATIQUE DU DROIT

Cette rubrique traite de la pratique du droit dans ses aspects de gestion des cabinets, principalement. Elle propose des ouvrages susceptibles de conseiller les membres de la profession dans l'exercice de leurs fonctions. Voir aussi : DISCIPLINAIRE (DROIT) et RESPONSABILITÉ PROFESSIONNELLE.

LUNDY, DEREK, GAVIN MacKENZIE, AND MARY V. NEWBURY	*Barristers & Solicitors in Practice*	LN/B (LL)
ADAMSKI, JAKUB	"Legal Profession," a vol. of *Halsbury's Law of Canada*, 1st ed.	LN/B 2007
COURNOYER, GUY *et al.*	*Code des professions annoté*	Y Blais 2007
LACROIX, MARIÈVE	*L'avocat diffamateur: ses devoirs de conduite et la mise en œuvre de sa responsabilité civile*	Y Blais 2007
HARDIE, ROBERT A.	*A Practical Guide to Successful Law Firm Management*	LN/B 2006
CRONK, ELEANOR A., AND E. SUSAN ELLIOTT	*Practice Essentials 2001*	LSUC 2001
ZWICKER, MILTON W.	*Developing and Managing a Successful Law Firm*	Crswl 1995
PLANT, ALBERT	*Making Money: The Business of Law*	CLB 1993

62.

LEGAL REASONING

It has been so frequently uttered that it borders on cliché, but many law schools in the common law world insist on stating that "we teach our students to think like lawyers." It is true that there is a distinct manner in which lawyers approach legal issues and problems as compared to most other disciplines. This list contains a number of Canadian works (in this case, nationality is immaterial) and one U.K. work which discuss the process of legal reasoning and problem-solving. Related topics: ADVOCACY, LEGAL RESEARCH, LEGAL THEORY, LEGAL WRITING.

INTERPRÉTATION DES LOIS

Les facultés de droit visent à former des juristes qui puissent penser correctement en droit. Le raisonnement juridique, en effet, comporte plusieurs caractéristiques propres qui le distingue des autres disciplines. Ce domaine ignore les frontières géographiques habituelles. Voir aussi : RECHERCHE DOCUMENTAIRE ; THÉORIE DU DROIT ; RÉDACTION JURIDIQUE.

FITZGERALD, MAUREEN F.	*Legal Problem Solving: Reasoning, Research & Writing*, 4th ed.	LN/B 2007
POIRIER, DONALD	*L'interprétation de la loi*	Université de Moncton 2006
MACCORMICK, NEIL	*Rhetoric and The Rule of Law: A Theory of Legal Reasoning* (U.K.)	OUP 2005
TREMBLAY, RICHARD	*L'essentiel de l'interprétation des lois*	Y Blais 2004
WADDAMS, STEPHEN M	*Introduction to the Study of Law*, 6th ed.	Crswl 2004
MCCALLUM, MARGARET E.	*Synthesis: Legal Reading, Reasoning, and Writing in Canada*, 2d ed.	CCH Cdn 2003
KWAW, EDMUND M.A.	*The Guide to Legal Analysis, Legal Methodology, and Legal Writing*	EM 1992

63.

LEGAL RESEARCH

Research is all too frequently undervalued and overlooked as a step in the suite of skills necessary for success in the legal profession. Fortunately, however, there is a healthy body of work devoted to imparting these very skills to busy lawyers, law students, and anyone with an interest in the law. Related topics: LEGAL REASONING, LEGAL WRITING.

RECHERCHE DOCUMENTAIRE

Une des méthodologies nécessaires au travail juridique. La recherche documentaire est envisagée ici sous l'angle général, car tout le présent ouvrage contribue à faciliter le travail de recherche dans les domaines abordés.

Le May, Denis	*La recherche documentaire en droit*, 6e éd.	W & LaF 2008
Iosipescu, Michael J., and Philip Whitehead	*Legal Writing and Research Manual*, 6th ed.	LN/B 2004
Tjaden, Ted	*Legal Research and Writing*, 2d ed.	Irwin 2004
MacEllven, Douglass T. *et al.*	*Legal Research Handbook*, 5th ed.	LN/B 2003
Castel, Jacqueline R., and Omeela K. Latchman	*The Practical Guide to Canadian Legal Research*, 2d ed.	Crswl 1996
Banks, Margaret A., and Karen E.H. Foti	*Banks on Using a Law Library: A Canadian Guide to Legal Research*, 6th ed.	Crswl 1994

64.

LEGAL SYSTEM

Works in this area provide information about the foundations and workings of our legal system, including Parliament, legislatures, courts, boards, and tribunals, etc. A number of titles deal with the "criminal justice" system, which should be viewed as a subset of the legal system in that it is essentially concerned with matters related only to criminal law and punishment and not the legal system in its entirety. Related topics: CIVIL PROCEDURE, CRIMINAL LAW, CRIMINAL PROCEDURE, and SENTENCING.

SYSTÈME JURIDIQUE

Cette rubrique n'est pas à proprement parler une division du droit mais une expression qui permet d'étudier le droit globalement. On trouve dans cette catégorie des ouvrages généraux et d'introduction sur le droit canadien ou québécois et une présentation des principales institutions juridiques. Voir aussi : PROCÉDURE CIVILE ; CRIMINEL (DROIT) ; PROCÉDURE PÉNALE et SENTENCES.

GAUDREAULT-DESBIENS, JEAN-FRANÇOIS	*Les solitudes du bijuridisme au Canada : essai sur les rapports de pouvoir entre les traditions juridiques et la résillience des atavismes identaires*	Thémis 2007
ATKINSON, PAUL	*The Canadian Justice System: An Overview*	LN/B 2005
FORCESE, CRAIG AND AARON FREEMAN	*The Laws of Government: The Legal Foundations of Canadian Democracy*	Irwin 2005
CANADA	*Le système de justice du Canada*	Ministère de la Justice, Direction des Communications 2005
RAMCHARAN, SUBHAS	*Law, Order and the Canadian Criminal Justice System*	Canadian Educators' Press 2005
GALL, GERALD L.	*The Canadian Legal System*, 5th ed.	Crswl 2004
KÉLADA, HENRI	*Précis de droit québécois*	SOQUIJ 2004
BOYD, NEIL	*Canadian Law: An Introduction*	Nelson Thomson Learning 2002
FITZGERALD, PATRICK, AND BARRY WRIGHT	*Looking at Law: Canada's Legal System*, 5th ed.	LN/B 2000
TREMBLAY, G.	*Une grille d'analyse pour le droit du Québec*, 3e éd.	W & LaF 1993

65.

LEGAL THEORY

Legal theory asks the question: "What is law?" Although the answer to this question might at first seem straightforward, it is a weighty issue that has engendered a torrent of written opinion and theorizing. Some view law as a "system of rules," others have seen law as fitting into larger matrixes and have thus developed other schools of thought (e.g., utilitarianism, legal positivism), while still others have theorized about law in other contexts (e.g., economic, sociological, feminist, etc.). This lists three Canadian titles in the field, and two from the United Kingdom. This is a topic in which nationality is essentially immaterial. Related topic: LEGAL REASONING.

THÉORIE DU DROIT

La recherche des concepts fondamentaux du droit, des liens entre les éléments du système juridique, la critique de l'idéologie juridique et la recherche d'une cohérence axiologique ou téléologique, sont autant de raisons de s'intéresser au vaste domaine de la théorie du droit. Ce domaine comprend, selon les définitions qu'on en donne, la philosophie du droit, l'épistémologie du droit et la méthodologie fondamentale. Il touche à la RÉDACTION JURIDIQUE, à l'INTERPRÉTATION DES LOIS et à la recherche en droit (autre que documentaire).

BICKENBACH, JEROME EDMUND	*Canadian Cases in the Philosophy of Law*, 4th ed.	Broadview Press 2007
DE COSTE, F.C.	*On Coming to Law: An Introduction to Law in Liberal Societies*, 2d ed.	LN/B 2007
GAUDREAULT-DESBIENS, JEAN-FRANÇOIS	*Les solitudes du bijuridisme au Canada : essai sur les rapports de pouvoir entre les traditions juridiques et la résillience des atavismes identaires*	Thémis 2007
MILLARD, ÉRIC	*Théorie générale du droit*	Dalloz (Paris) 2006
WARD, IAN	*Introduction to Critical Legal Theory*, 2d ed. (U.K.)	Cavendish 2004
BERGEL, JEAN-LOUIS	*Théorie générale du droit*	Dalloz (Paris) 2003
DEVLIN, RICHARD F.	*Canadian Perspectives on Legal Theory*	EM 1991
DEVLIN, RICHARD F.	*Critical Legal Studies*	EM 1991

66.

LEGAL WRITING

Lawyers are communicators. Whether through oral advocacy or in the production of written memoranda-of-law and opinion pieces, lawyers are constantly called upon to communicate clearly, logically, succinctly, and effectively. They are also called upon to produce written documents that are very specific to the profession, for example, pleadings and contracts, *inter alia*. There are numerous works devoted to assisting lawyers (and law students) to become better writers. Related topic: LEGAL RESEARCH.

RÉDACTION JURIDIQUE

C'est une des méthodologies du travail juridique. Le droit étant un média écrit, savoir écrire devient nécessaire à tous les stades du développement des normes juridiques. Si les principes rédactionnels juridiques sont assez communs à l'ensemble des genres littéraires juridiques, il est d'usage et commode de distinguer la rédaction législative, contractuelle, procédurale et judiciaire.

BEAULNE, JACQUES ET CHAMBRE DES NOTAIRES DU QUÉBEC	La rédaction des testaments notariés	Chambre des notaires du Québec 2007
TÉTRAULT, MICHEL	La rédaction des conventions en matière familiale	Y Blais 2007
ALBERT, MARIE-FRANCE	Le style de la common law	Y Blais 2005
MERCIER, CARL	Guide de rédaction juridique	Centre collégial de développement de matériel didactique 2005
TREMBLAY, SERGE	Rédaction d'une convention collective : guide d'initiation	Presses de l'Université du Québec 2005
IOSIPESCU, MICHAEL J., AND PHILIP WHITEHEAD	Legal Writing and Research Manual, 6th ed.	LN/B 2004
MAILHOT, LOUISE	Écrire la décision : guide pratique de rédaction judiciaire	Y Blais 2004
TJADEN, TED	Legal Research and Writing, 2d ed.	Irwin 2004
GENDREAU, YSOLDE	Le lisible et l'illisible / The Legible and the Illegible	Thémis 2003
McCALLUM, MARGARET E.	Synthesis: Legal Reading, Reasoning, and Writing in Canada, 2d ed.	CCH Cdn 2003
GORDON, SUZANNE	The Law Workbook: Developing Skills for Legal Research and Writing	EM 2001

Mowat, Christine	*A Plain Language Handbook for Legal Writers*	Crswl 1998
Driedger, Elmer A.	*A Manual of Instructions for Legislative and Legal Writing*	Canadian Department of Justice 1982

- LETTRES DE CHANGE voir BILLS OF EXCHANGE
- LOGEMENT LOCATIF (LOUAGE) voir LANDLORD & TENANT
- LOUAGE voir LANDLORD & TENANT
- MAGISTRATURE voir COURTS
- MANDAT voir AGENCY

67.

MARITIME LAW

Also referred to as "Admiralty Law," this is the law of ships and shipping, including navigation and harbours and other matters related to shipping. In Canada this is an area of almost exclusively federal jurisdiction by way of the *Canada Shipping Act.* Related topic: TRANSPORTATION LAW.

MARITIME (DROIT)

Le droit maritime comporte des aspects de droit ADMINISTRATIF et de droit des TRANSPORTS. Ce qui le rend complexe, c'est, d'une part, le partage des compétences fédérales (transport interprovincial et international) et provinciales (transport local) et, d'autre part, le recours au droit INTERNATIONAL PUBLIC. Le transport maritime international repose principalement sur de grandes conventions internationales auxquelles le Canada a adhéré. Dans l'écosystème juridique, on fera des nuances entre le droit de la mer, plus englobant (dont l'importante convention de 1982 sur le droit de la mer) et le droit maritime, plus près du droit des AFFAIRES.

BOURGEOIS, MARC A.	*Le droit maritime*	Université de Moncton 2005
BÉDARD, CHARLES	*Le bassin du Saint-Laurent et les Grands Lacs: cadre juridique*	Presses de l'Université Laval 2004
FORUM DE CONCERTATION SUR LE TRANSPORT MARITIME (QUÉBEC), GROUPE DE TRAVAIL SUR LE CABOTAGE	*Situation actuelle et perspectives du cabotage au Québec* [ressource électronique]	Québec, Forum de concertation sur le transport maritime 2003
GOLD, EDGAR	*Maritime Law*	Irwin 2003
FERNANDES, RUI M.	*Shipping and Admiralty Law*	Crswl 1995
FERNANDES, RUI M.	*The Annotated* Canada Shipping Act	LN/B 1988
JOHNSTON, DOUGLAS M.	*Canada and the New International Law of the Sea*	U of T Press 1985
LAW SOCIETY OF UPPER CANADA	*Marine Law in General Practice*	LSUC 1980

◆   MARQUES DE COMMERCE voir TRADE-MARKS

68.

MILITARY LAW

This is the internal law of the Canadian Armed Forces dealing with discipline of its members. It is entirely federal in scope by way of the *National Defence Act*, which sets out the procedural rules to be employed and acts as a "criminal code" for members of the Forces. Related topics: CIVIL PROCEDURE, CRIMINAL LAW, CRIMINAL PROCEDURE, HUMAN RIGHTS AND THE *CHARTER OF RIGHTS AND FREEDOMS*.

MILITAIRE (DROIT)

Domaine de compétence législative fédérale, le droit militaire couvre une foule de questions variées et complexes : les bases militaires, le statut de l'armée et des soldats, les lois applicables aux plans civil, criminel, disciplinaire, etc. Faute d'ouvrages abondants sur la question, on se rappellera que le domaine est abordé en droit CONSTITUTIONNEL. S'agissant de droit public, on peut compléter en droit anglais. La question du comportement humanitaire en temps de guerre est réglée dans des conventions internationales (dont celles dites « de Genève ») auxquelles le Canada a adhéré.

Létourneau, Gilles, and Michael W. Drapeau	*Canadian Military Law Annotated*	Crswl 2006
Emanuelli, Claude	*Les Casques bleus : policiers ou combattants ?*	W & LaF 1997
Simpson, James M.	*Droit applicable aux Forces canadiennes en Somalie en 1992–1993 : étude préparée pour la Commission d'enquête sur le déploiement des Forces canadiennes en Somalie*	La Commission 1997
Watkin, Kenneth W., and Roxanne Neufeld	"Armed Forces" in vol. 1A, title 9 of the *Canadian Encyclopedic Digest* (Ontario) and vol. 2, title 9 of the *Canadian Encyclopedic Digest* (Western)	Crswl 1991
Swainson, Arthur K.	*The Rules of Evidence at Courts Martial: A Study of the Military Rules of Evidence*	U of Man, Faculty of Law (thesis) 1976
Fay, James B.	*Canadian Military Criminal Law: An Examination of Military Justice*	Dalhousie University (thesis) 1974
Singer, Burrell M.	*Handbook of Canadian Military Law*	Copp Clark 1941

MORTGAGES & LIENS

"A mortgage is a conveyance of land or an assignment of chattels as security for the payment of a debt or for the discharge of some other obligation . . . ." (*Santley v. White*, [1899] 2 Ch. 474 (C.A.)) A lien is similar to a mortgage but "can only attach to property which is or has been the subject of a transaction between parties. . . ." (R.S. Vasan, ed., *The Canadian Law Dictionary*, New York: Law and Business Publications, 1980)) Liens are most frequently used by builders, warehouses, and mechanics. These are topics that are provincial in jurisdiction. Related topics: PERSONAL PROPERTY SECURITY, PROPERTY, REAL PROPERTY.

PRIORITÉS ET HYPOTHÈQUES

Branche importante du droit civil couvrant l'ancien domaine des sûretés (privilèges, hypothèques, nantissements, etc.). La réforme du *Code civil* est majeure dans ce domaine (hypothèques mobilières, ouvertes, etc.) de sorte que de nombreuses anciennes règles n'ont plus cours. Les dispositions transitoires, ici plus qu'ailleurs, doivent être consultées. Le contrat de cautionnement est rapatrié avec les contrats nommés. Voir aussi : PERSONAL PROPERTY SECURITY.

BRISTOW, DAVID I., AND DOUGLAS W. MACKLEM	*Construction Builders' and Mechanics' Liens in Canada*, 7th ed.	Crswl (LL)
TRAUB, WALTER M.	*Falconbridge on Mortgages*, 5th ed.	CLB (LL)
PAYETTE, LOUIS	*Les sûretés réelles dans le* Code civil du Québec	Y Blais 2006
SARNA, LAZAR	*The law of immovable hypothecs in Québec*	LN/B 2006
PRATTE, DENISE	*Priorités et hypothèques*	Éditions Revue de droit, Université de Sherbrooke 2005
REID, JULIEN	*Code des sûretés*	W & LaF 2005
JACQUES, LOUISE	*Les recours hypothécaires*	Y Blais 2003
LACHAPELLE, LUCIEN	*Hypothèques, etc. : aspects théoriques, critiques et pratiques*	À compte d'auteur 2003
DURBIN, EDWIN Z.	"Mortgages" in vol. 21, title 96 of the *Canadian Encyclopedic Digest* (Ontario)	Crswl 1995
ROACH, JOSEPH E.	*The Canadian Law of Mortgages of Land*	LN/B 1993

MOTOR VEHICLE LAW

Canada is a country of vast distances, most of which are traversed by motor vehicle. This topic concerns the law as it applies to these vehicles (cars, trucks, motorcycles, etc.). It is a matter of mostly provincial jurisdiction, by way of the various provincial highway traffic codes. There is some federal involvement, however, in that there are number of offences in the *Criminal Code* that deal with the operation of a motor vehicle (e.g., dangerous operation at section 249, operation while impaired at section 253, and failure to remain at the scene of an accident at section 252). Most of the titles under this topic deal with motor vehicle related crimes. Related topics: CRIMINAL LAW, INSURANCE LAW, NEGLIGENCE, TRANSPORTATION LAW.

VÉHICULES AUTOMOBILES

L'immensité du pays explique en grande partie l'usage de l'automobile. Ce domaine juridique qui couvre les véhicules (autos, motos, camions), est principalement de juridiction provinciale. Certaines infractions graves sont bien entendu du domaine criminel cf. aa. 249, 252 et 253 C. Cr. relatifs à la conduite dangereuse, avec facultés affaiblies ou l'omission de demeurer sur les lieux d'un accident. La plupart des ouvrages cités ice concernent ces aspects. Voir aussi : CRIMINEL (DROIT) ; ASSURANCES ; RESPONSABILITÉ CIVILE et TRANSPORTS (DROIT DES).

McLeod, R.M., Judge J.D.Takach, and Murray D. Segal	*Breathalyzer Law in Canada: The Prosecution and Defence of Drinking and Driving Offences*, 3d ed.	Crswl (LL)
McLeod, R.M., Justice J.D.Takach, and Murray D. Segal	Criminal Code *Driving Offences*	Crswl (LL)
Segal, Murray D.	*The Manual of Motor Vehicle Law*, 3d ed.	Crswl (LL)
Lamoureux, Marie-Hélène et Alain Bissonnette	*Code de la sécurité routière annoté, 2008: lois et règlements connexes*	Y Blais 2007
Kenkel, Justice Joseph F.	*Impaired Driving in Canada*	LN/B 2006
Perreault, Janick	*L'indemnisation du préjudice corporel des victimes d'accident d'automobile*, 2e éd.	CCH 2005
Hutchison, Scott D., David Rose, and Phillip Downes	*The Law of Traffic Offences*, 2d ed.	Crswl 1998

71.

MUNICIPAL LAW

Municipalities are creations of provincial statute and have limited powers with regard to taxation, zoning, and other matters normally dealt with at the local level. A major legal activity within the municipal sphere is that related to planning. Related topics: ADMINISTRATIVE LAW, POLICE & PRIVATE SECURITY LAW, REAL PROPERTY, TAXATION.

MUNICIPAL (DROIT)

Branche du droit public, le droit municipal couvre un grand nombre de problèmes juridiques à un niveau décentralisé par rapport à la législature. Ce domaine est grandement investi des nouvelles pratiques en aménagement et urbanisme ainsi qu'en ENVIRONNEMENT. La complexité du domaine tient aux nombreux paliers d'intervention autant qu'au degré de détail des questions posées. Les élections font l'objet d'une législation distincte.

ROGERS, IAN MACFEE	*Canadian Law of Planning and Zoning*, 2d ed.	Crswl (LL)
QUÉBEC	*Code des municipalités*	CCH 2006
QUÉBEC	Loi sur les compétences municipales *et* Loi sur les cités et villes : *textes explicatifs et références législatives*	CCH 2006
ST-AMOUR, JEAN-PIERRE	*Le droit municipal de l'urbanisme discrétionnaire au Québec*	Y Blais 2006
GALLAND, GHISLAIN	*La gestion des droits acquis à l'usage, en droit municipal québécois*	Université Laval, Faculté de droit 2004
MAKUCH, STANLEY, NEIL CRAIK, AND SIGNE B. LEISK	*Canadian Municipal and Planning Law*, 2d ed.	Crswl 2004
HÉTU, JEAN	*Droit municipal : principes généraux et contentieux*, 2e éd.	CCH 2003
MACLEAN, VIRGINIA, AND THOMAS RICHARDSON	*A User's Guide to Municipal By-Laws*	LN/B 2001
HILLEL, DAVID	*Thomson Rogers on Municipal Liability*	CLB 1996
ROGERS, IAN MACFEE	*The Law of Canadian Municipal Corporations*, 2d ed.	Crswl 1988

72.

NEGLIGENCE

This huge portion of tort law deals with acts (or omissions) that cause harm to others. Normally, for negligence to be proved a plaintiff must show that the defendant had some responsibility to take care not to harm the plaintiff (duty of care), that what the defendant did (or failed to do) which caused the harm was not what a reasonable person would have done (standard of care), and, finally, that the plaintiff did, in fact, suffer some injury from the defendant's action. Some negligent acts, however, can be proved without reference to the above test. This type of negligence is referred to as absolute or strict liability. There are also certain negligent acts that constitute a crime (i.e., criminal negligence). This is an area of the law that is rooted primarily in jurisprudence. All major works on torts also contain chapters devoted to negligence. Related topics: CLASS ACTIONS, CRIMINAL LAW, DAMAGES, EVIDENCE (CIVIL), HEALTH LAW, NUISANCE, OCCUPIER'S LIABILITY, PRODUCTS LIABILITY, REMEDIES & RESTITUTION, TORTS.

RESPONSABILITÉ CIVILE

Branche majeure du droit civil et partie importante du domaine des OBLIGATIONS.

PHILIPS-NOOTENS, SUZANNE *et al.*	*Éléments de responsabilité civile médicale,* 3e éd.	Y Blais 2007
WALTON, JUDGE CHRISTOPHER *et al.*	*Charlesworth & Percy on Negligence,* 11th ed. (U.K.)	S & M 2006
BÉLANGER-HARDY, LOUISE	*La responsabilité délictuelle en common law*	Y Blais 2005
BUCKLEY, R.A.	*The Law of Negligence,* 4th ed. (U.K.)	LN/B 2005
BAUDOUIN, JEAN-LOUIS	*La responsabilité civile*	Y Blais 2003
LINDEN, ALLEN M.	*La responsabilité civile délictuelle*	Centre franco-ontarien de ressources pédagogiques 2001
FELDTHUSEN, BRUCE	*Economic Negligence: The Recovery of Pure Economic Loss,* 4th ed.	Crswl 2000
LEVINSON, RICHARD E.	"Negligence" in vol. 23, title 101 of the *Canadian Encyclopedic Digest* (Ontario) and vol. 25, title 102 of the *Canadian Encyclopedic Digest* (Western)	Crswl 2000
ROCCAMO, GIOVANNA *et al.*	*Personal Injury Actions*	Crswl 1994

NAFTA (NORTH AMERICAN FREE TRADE AGREEMENT)

Canada is signator to a number of bilateral and multilateral trade agreements, but none is as significant as the *North American Free Trade Agreement* between Canada, the United States of America, and Mexico. *NAFTA* was an extension of an earlier bilateral treaty between Canada and the U.S. (known simply as "The Free Trade Agreement"). As Canada is very much an exporting nation (and a huge percentage of its export trade is with the United States), this is an extremely important pact with an enormous effect upon Canada's economy. As this trade pact involves two other countries, there are non-Canadian titles worthy of inclusion. Related topics: COMMERCIAL ARBITRATION, INTERNATIONAL SALE OF GOODS, INTERNATIONAL TRADE LAW.

ALENA (ACCORD DE LIBRE-ÉCHANGE NORD-AMÉRICAIN)

Vaste domaine couvrant plus de la moitié des branches du droit. On utilise cette expression pour désigner l'ensemble des dimensions juridiques applicables à la conduite des affaires («*doing business*»). L'expression « Droit commercial » tend à disparaître avec le nouveau Code civil du Québec. Plusieurs aspects du droit des affaires font l'objet d'une rubrique distincte : BANCAIRE (DROIT), COMMERCIAL INTERNATIONAL (DROIT), COMPAGNIES, CONCURRENCE (DROIT DE LA), CONSOMMATEUR, FAILLITE ET INSOLVABILITÉ, FISCALITÉ, FRANCHISE, LETTRES DE CHANGE, COPROPRIÉTE ; SOCIÉTÉS ET ASSOCIATIONS et VALEURS MOBILIÈRES. Il s'ensuit que tout ouvrage qui porte sur l'ensemble du droit des affaires ne peut être considéré que comme une introduction.

CURTIS, JOHN M. ET AARON SYDOR	L'ALENA : *déjà dix ans*	Affaires étrangères et Commerce international Canada, 2006
AZUELOS, MARTINE *et al.*	*Intégration dans les Amériques : dix ans d'ALENA*	Presses de la Sorbonne nouvelle 2004
DAUZIER, MARTINE	*Le Mexique face aux États-Unis : stratégies et changements dans le cadre de l'ALENA*	L'Harmattan 2004
CAMERON, MAXWELL A. AND BRIAN W. TOMLIN	*The Making of* NAFTA : *How the Deal was Done* (U.S.)	Cornell University Press 2000
LEMIEUX, DENIS	*Review of Administrative Action under* NAFTA	Crswl 1999
TREFLER, DANIEL	*The Long and Short of the Canada-U.S. Free Trade Agreement*	Industry Canada 1999
JOHNSON, JON R.	*International Trade Law*	Irwin 1998
APPLETON, BARRY	*Navigating* NAFTA : *A Concise User's Guide to the* North American Free Trade Agreement	Crswl 1994
LIVINGSTON TRADE SERVICES	*Livingston's* NAFTA *Handbook : Canadian Customs Procedures*	Crswl 1994

74.

NUISANCE

A specific subset of tort law, Nuisance is an act (or omission) by one party that affects another party's ability to use and enjoy their property, or negatively affects their comfort or health. There are two major divisions within this topic: private nuisance (where the affected party is an individual or specific individuals) and public nuisance (where the public is affected generally). Examples of nuisance include noise, smells, smoke, etc. There is also criminal nuisance (which is always a public nuisance) by virtue of section 180 of the *Criminal Code*. There are numerous municipal by-laws that deal with nuisance (e.g., anti-noise ordinances), and most provinces have a statute dealing with nuisance and a number have other enactments enabling certain agricultural operations to engage in activities that might otherwise be considered to be a nuisance with immunity from legal action. Related topics: AGRICULTURAL & AQUACULTURE LAW, CRIMINAL LAW, MUNICIPAL LAW, REAL PROPERTY, TORTS.

RESPONSABILITÉ CIVILE

Branche majeure du droit civil et partie importante du domaine des OBLIGATIONS.

OSBORNE, PHILIP H.	"Nuisance," chapter 6 in *The Law of Torts*, 3d ed.	Irwin 2007
BARREAU DU QUÉBEC	*Les dommages en matière civile et commerciale*	Y Blais 2006
LINDEN, JUSTICE ALLEN, AND BRUCE FELDTHUSEN	"Nuisance," chapter 15 in *Canadian Tort Law*, 8th ed.	LN/B 2006
BÉLANGER-HARDY, LOUISE	*La responsabilité délictuelle en common law*	Y Blais 2005
BAUDOUIN, JEAN-LOUIS	*La responsabilité civile*	Y Blais 2003
MALCOLM, ROSALIND, AND JOHN POINTING	*Statutory Nuisance: Law and Practice* (U.K.)	OUP 2003
FRIDMAN, GERALD H.L.	"Nuisance," chapter 8 in *The Law of Torts in Canada*, 2d ed.	Crswl 2002
PROCTOR, ROGER W.	"Nuisance" in vol. 23, title 102 of the *Canadian Encyclopedic Digest* (Ontario)	Crswl 1999
McCONNELL, MOIRA, AND ERIKA GERLOCK	*Environmental Spills: Emergency Reporting, Clean-up, and Liability* [separate titles for Alberta, British Columbia, and Ontario]	Crswl 1995

75.

OCCUPATIONAL HEALTH & SAFETY

This area of the law, the intent of which is to protect Canadian workers from needless danger in the workplace, is one of mixed federal and provincial jurisdiction. For the most part, provincial health and safety legislation governs workplaces that are subject to provincial regulation, while some specific federal statutes govern some industries (e.g., the *Atomic Energy Control Act,* which applies in all workplaces involved in the provision of atomic energy). A major component of this area of law is WHMIS (Workplace Hazardous Materials Information System). WHMIS is an initiative that was collaboratively undertaken by the federal government, the provinces, and major labour unions to ensure that workers are aware of any and all hazardous materials in their workplace and to keep current all information in the workplace about the handling of hazardous materials. Related topics: EMPLOYMENT LAW, ENVIRONMENTAL LAW, HUMAN RESOURCES LAW, LABOUR LAW, NUISANCE, TRANSPORTATION LAW.

SANTÉ ET SÉCURITÉ AU TRAVAIL

Vaste et important domaine du droit public et ADMINISTRATIF (par son côté organisationnel), la SST appartient au droit du TRAVAIL, car le travail en fournit le contexte d'application. Il tient cependant plutôt des régimes de sécurité sociale dont il est une espèce. Voir aussi : ACCIDENTS DU TRAVAIL ET MALADIES PROFESSIONNELLES.

Ferguson, Reg	*WHMIS Compliance Manual*	Crswl (LL)
Keith, Norman A.	*Canadian Health & Safety Law: A Comprehensive Guide to the Statutes, Policies, and Case Law*	CLB (LL)
Drapeau, Murielle	*Questions et réponses en santé et sécurité au travail*	CCH 2007
Québec	*Règlement annoté sur le barème des dommages corporels*	CSST 2006
Keith, Norman A.	*Workplace Health & Safety Crimes*	LN/B 2004
Kell, Laura	"Occupational Health & Safety" in vol. 23, title 102.1 of the *Canadian Encyclopedic Digest* (Ontario)	Crswl 1995
Simon, Paul L.S.	*Hazardous Products: Canada's Right-to-Know Laws*	CCH Cdn 1987

76.

OCCUPIER'S LIABILITY

Another subset of tort law (specifically of negligence), this topic deals with the legal responsibilities of property owners and occupiers (tenants) to ensure that their premises are free from potential dangers to visitors. An example of a garden variety occupier's liability case would be a slip-and-fall-suit because of a wet floor, or because of an icy sidewalk leading to the premises. This is an area of provincial concern and is heavily rooted in caselaw. Related topics: NEGLIGENCE, TORTS.

RESPONSABILITÉ CIVILE

Branche majeure du droit civil et partie importante du domaine des OBLIGATIONS.

WAGNER, ERIC J.	*The Annotated British Columbia* Occupier's Liability Act	CLB (LL)
OSBORNE, PHILIP H.	"Occupiers' Liability," Part E in chapter 3 of *The Law of Torts*, 3d ed.	Irwin 2007
LINDEN, JUSTICE ALLEN, AND BRUCE FELDTHUSEN	"Occupier's Liability," chapter 18 in *Canadian Tort Law*, 8th ed.	LN/B 2006
BÉLANGER-HARDY, LOUISE	*La responsabilité délictuelle en common law*	Y Blais 2005
BAUDOUIN, JEAN-LOUIS	*La responsabilité civile*	Y Blais 2003
KLAR, LEWIS N.	"Occupier's Liability," chapter 15 in *Tort Law*, 3d edition	Crswl 2003
LEVINSON, RICHARD E.	"Occupier's Liability," Part IV in "Negligence" in vol. 23, title 101 of the *Canadian Encyclopedic Digest* (Ontario) and in vol. 25, title 102 of the *Canadian Encyclopedic Digest* (Western)	Crswl 2000

77.

PARTNERSHIPS

This is the common business arrangement whereby two or more parties enter into a commercial arrangement with a view to generating profit. The existence of a partnership will normally be signified by express declaration (e.g., a written partnership agreement) or it can be inferred by conduct that demonstrates the existence of a partnership. The commercial landscape is becoming increasingly more populated by LLPs (limited liability partnerships), which are partnerships that have taken on some of the characteristics of corporations. This is an area of provincial jurisdiction. Most provinces have legislation dealing with partnerships and some (e.g., Ontario) have a specific act devoted to limited partnerships. Related topics: COMMERCIAL LAW, CONTRACTS, CORPORATE LAW.

SOCIÉTÉS ET ASSOCIATIONS

Contrats nommés prévus au *Code civil*, la société et l'association constituent un des principaux moyens de regroupement des personnes en dehors des mécanismes des personnes morales (COMPAGNIES). La société formée pour la conduite des affaires est étudiée également dans les ouvrages de droit des AFFAIRES bien que, souvent, de façon sommaire.

Manzer, Alison R.	*A Practical Guide to Canadian Partnership Law*	CLB (LL)
Larochelle, Bernard	*Contrat de société et d'association*	W & LaF 2007
Harris, Doug *et al.*	*Cases, Materials, and Notes on Partnership and Canadian Business Corporations*, 4th ed.	Crswl 2004
Van Duzer, Anthony	*The Law of Partnerships and Corporations*, 2d ed.	Irwin 2003
Swartz, L. Brian	"Partnership" in vol. 24, title 106 of the *Canadian Encyclopedic Digest* (Ontario)	Crswl 2002
Labrecque, Marc-André et Denis Racine	*Les principales formes juridiques de l'entreprise au Québec*	Les Publications du Québec 2000
Thériault, Michelle	*L'exercice de la profession d'avocat avec d'autres: quel contrat choisir ?*	BQ, Service de l'inspection professionnelle 1998
Hepburn, Lyle R., and William J. Strain	*Limited Partnerships 1996*	Crswl 1996

78.

PATENTS

A patent is the legal protection given to a functional idea (i.e., the creation of an original product or process). This is a particular topic within intellectual property. Patents are granted by the federal government by way of the Patent Office (which is a division of the Department of Industry) under the authority of the *Patent Act*. Related topics: COMMERCIAL LAW, INTELLECTUAL PROPERTY LAW.

BREVETS

Domaine particulier de la propriété intellectuelle, dont il constitue un pilier avec le DROIT D'AUTEUR et celui des MARQUES DE COMMERCE, le droit des brevets porte sur la protection spécifique des inventions. Ce domaine, jadis confiné au monde industriel, s'est graduellement étendu aux produits agricoles, ainsi qu'à la matière vivante.

HUGHES, JUSTICE ROGER T., DINO P. CLARIZIO, AND NEAL ARMSTRONG	*Hughes & Woodley on Patents*, 2d ed.	LN/B (LL)
GERVAIS, DANIEL J.	*Le droit de la propriété intellectuelle*	Crswl 2006
HUGHES, JUSTICE ROGER T.	*Patent Legislation and Commentary*, 2006–07 edition	LN/B 2006
KRATZ, MARTIN P.J.	*Obtaining Patents*	Crswl 1999
VAVER, DAVID	"Patents," chapter 3 in *Intellectual Property Law: Copyright, Patents, and Trade-Marks*	Irwin 1997
HENDERSON, GORDON F.	*Patent Law of Canada*	Crswl 1994

79.

PENSIONS

The provision of payment to former and retired employees comes in a variety of forms, all of which are often collectively referred to as pensions. There are public pensions, such as the Canada Pension Plan, to which all workers in Canada contribute (the exception being in Québec where the Québec Pension Plan stands in its place), and the Old Age Pension, the benefit of which is conferred upon all Canadians upon reaching the age of 65 years. These are federal schemes and are governed by federal legislation. There are also private pensions from employers or by way of self-contributed schemes (e.g., RSPs). This topic is one of mixed jurisdiction in that pensions are largely provincial in domain, but there are significant agreements between the provinces and federal government and there is pension legislation in each of the provinces. Related topics: EMPLOYMENT LAW, LABOUR LAW, TAXATION (INCOME TAX).

RÉGIMES DE RETRAITE

Réalité de plus en plus importante, compte tenu du vieillissement de la population, la retraite se situe au carrefour de plusieurs questions juridiques. Les régimes publics (fédéraux comme provinciaux) participent d'une politique de sécurité sociale. Les régimes privés empruntent et complètent les règles des ASSURANCES ; ils font l'objet d'un CONTRAT, parfois d'un contrat nommé, appelé rente, s'insèrent souvent dans un projet de planification fiscale (voir : FISCALITÉ) et deviennent objets de SUCCESSIONS.

Mercer Human Resource Consulting	*The Mercer Pension Manual*	Crswl (LL)
Albert, Jean-Paul et Simon Descôteaux	*Guide sur le partage des régimes de retraite au Québec*, 2e éd.	CCH 2007
Albert, Jean-Paul	*Guide sur les régimes de retraite et les avantages sociaux au Québec*	CCH 2006
Kaplan, Ari N.	*Pension Law*	Irwin 2006
Seller, Susan G.	*Federal Pension Legislation*, 2006–07 ed.	CLB 2006
Knight, Jamie, and Matthew Vella	Canada Pension Plan Act *and* Québec Pension Plan Act: *A Quick Reference*, 2005 ed.	Crswl 2005
Francis, Heidi H., and Christel Francis	"Pensions and Retirement Benefits" in vol. 25, title 108 of the *Canadian Encyclopedic Digest* (Ontario)	Crswl 1997

80.

PERSONAL PROPERTY SECURITY

Growing out of chattel mortgages, the use of one's personal property in order to secure (guarantee) a loan is referred to as personal property security. It is an area of provincial jurisdiction and most provinces have a personal property security act, but cases involving personal property security often venture into the federal sphere when a bankruptcy or insolvency are involved. Related topics: CONSTRUCTION LAW, CONTRACTS, DEBTOR & CREDITOR, MORTGAGES & LIENS, REMEDIES & RESTITUTION.

PRIORITÉS ET HYPOTHÈQUES

Branche importante du droit civil couvrant l'ancien domaine des sûretés (privilèges, hypothèques, nantissements, etc.). La réforme du *Code civil* est majeure dans ce domaine (hypothèques mobilières, ouvertes, etc.) de sorte que de nombreuses anciennes règles n'ont plus cours. Les dispositions transitoires, ici plus qu'ailleurs, doivent être consultées. Le contrat de cautionnement est rapatrié avec les contrats nommés.

McLaren, Richard H.	*Secured Transactions in Personal Property in Canada*, 2d cd.	Crswl (LL)
Beauchamp, François *et al.*	*Contrats, sûretés et publicité des droits*	Y Blais 2007
Bennett, Frank	*Bennett on the* Personal Property Security Act *(Ontario)*, 3d ed.	LN/B 2006
Payette, Louis	*Les sûretés réelles dans le Code civil du Québec*, 3e éd.	Y Blais 2006
Stikeman Elliott LLP	*Ontario* Personal Property Security Act & Commentary	LN/B 2006
Cuming, Ronald C.C., Catherine Walsh, and Roderick J. Wood	*Personal Property Security Law*	Irwin 2005
Pratte, Denise	*Priorités et hypothèques*, 2e éd.	Université de Sherbrooke 2005
Reid, Julien	*Code des sûretés*	W & LaF 2005
McLaren, Richard H.	"Secured Personal Property" in vol. 29, title 131 of the *Canadian Encyclopedic Digest* (Ontario)	Crswl 2003
Ziegel, Jacob S., Ronald Cuming, and Anthony J. Duggan	*Secured Transactions in Personal Property and Suretyships*, 4th ed.	EM 2003

+ PERSONNE (DROITS DE LA) voir HUMAN RIGHTS AND THE *CHARTER OF RIGHTS AND FREEDOMS*

81.

POLICE & PRIVATE SECURITY LAW

These titles deal with the law as it relates to policing in Canada and the provision of security services in the private sector. It also includes titles of interest to members of the police force and practitioners of private security services. This is largely an area of provincial concern, although there is one national police force—The Royal Canadian Mounted Police. Related topics: CRIMINAL LAW, CRIMINAL PROCEDURE, EVIDENCE (CRIMINAL), HUMAN RIGHTS AND THE *CHARTER OF RIGHTS AND FREEDOMS*, MUNICIPAL LAW.

POLICE

Branche sous-développée du droit public, malgré le fait que la police fasse l'objet de nombreuses réglementations. Rappelons le partage constitutionnel entre le fédéral et les provinces ainsi que la grande variété de corps policiers et parapoliciers (agences de sécurité, etc.). En tant que corps organisé dans l'État, la police relève du droit ADMINISTRATIF, les pouvoirs des policiers en matière de criminalité sont étudiés en droit CRIMINEL, en PROCÉDURE PÉNALE, etc.

DUNLOP, JOAN	"Police" in vol. 26, title 113 of the *Canadian Encyclopedic Digest* (Ontario)	Crswl 2006
NADEAU, ALAIN-ROBERT	*Annotated* Royal Canadian Mounted Police Act *and Regulations*	Y Blais 2006
BOUCHER, SUSANNE, AND KENNETH LANDA	*Understanding Section 8: Search Seizure, and the Canadian Constitution*	Irwin 2005
RAY, DAVID L.	*A Security Professional's Practical Guide to the Law*	CLB 2004
FONTANA, JAMES, AND DAVID KEESHAN	*Police Guide to Search and Seizure*, 5th ed.	LN/B 2003
GROOT, NORMAN J.	*Canadian Law and Private Investigations*	Irwin 2001
DUBOIS, KARINE	*L'arbitrage de différend chez les policiers et pompiers municipaux du Québec*	Université Laval 2000 (thèse)
SMITH, KENNETH R., AND ROBERT J. PROUSE	*Canadian Private Security Manual*, revised edition	Crswl 1989

- ◆ PREUVE CIVIL voir EVIDENCE (CIVIL)
- ◆ PREUVE PÉNALE voir EVIDENCE (CRIMINAL)
- ◆ PRIORITÉS ET HYPOTHÈQUES voir MORTGAGES & LIENS; PERSONAL PROPERTY SECURITY

82.

PRISON LAW

This topic deals with the laws governing corrections and correctional institutions. Jurisdiction is shared between the federal government (who have responsibility for penitentiaries) and the provinces (prisons and jails). More can be found on this topic in the areas of penology, criminology, and sociology than in law. Related topics: CRIMINAL LAW, SENTENCING, YOUNG OFFENDERS.

CARCÉRAL

On traite ici du système dans l'ensemble et des droits des prisonniers. Rappelons que la *Loi constitutionnelle de 1867* partage les competences entre le fédéral (pénitenciers, peine de plus de 2 ans) et les provinces (prisons, peines inférieures à 2 ans). Les grands ouvrages de droit criminel ou de droit pénal abordent parfois ces questions. Devant la pauvreté relative des références, on élargira la recherche à la criminologie en général; pour les peines et les sentences, voir: SENTENCES.

CONROY, JOHN W., AND EVA KOSSUTH	*Canadian Prison Law*	LN/B (LL)
MANDEL, MICHAEL	"Prisons" in vol. 27, title 116 of the *Canadian Encyclopedic Digest* (Ontario) and vol. 28, title 118 of the *Canadian Encyclopedic Digest* (Western)	Crswl 2004
HANNAH-MOFFAT, KELLY	*Punishment in Disguise: Penal Governance and Federal Imprisonment of Women in Canada*	U of T Press 2001
LEMONDE, LUCIE	*L'habeas corpus en droit carcéral*	Y Blais 1990
EKSTEDT, JOHN	*Corrections in Canada: Policy and Practice*, 2d ed.	LN/B 1988
GROUPE DE TRAVAIL SUR LA RÉVISION DU DROIT CORRECTIONEL	*Les autorités correctionnelles et les droits des détenus / Correctional Authority and Inmate Rights*	Canada (Solicitor-General) 1987
PLECAS, DARRYL B.	*Federal Corrections in Canada: A Comprehensive Introduction*	Good 80's Enterprises 1986

PRIVACY LAW & ACCESS TO INFORMATION

These two topics, which are frequently grouped together, relate to different ends of the information availability spectrum. Privacy law deals with the right of individuals to keep information about themselves private and, in cases where it must be disclosed to certain parties, the obligations on second parties to ensure that the information is not disclosed unnecessarily to third parties. Access to information, on the other hand, refers to the rights of citizens and organizations to see information created and held by the various levels of government in the process of governing. Both the federal and provincial levels of government are subject to access to information legislation and most provinces have statutes protecting the privacy rights of its citizens. Related topics: ADMINISTRATIVE LAW, HEALTH LAW, HUMAN RESOURCES LAW.

ACCÈS À L'INFORMATION

Ce domaine comporte deux principales dimensions : l'accès à un document détenu par un organisme et l'accès du citoyen à des informations le concernant, détenues par un organisme public ou une entreprise privée. La protection de la vie privée est couverte par le *Code Civil du Québec*. Le fédéral et le Québec ont tous deux légiféré. Le droit de l'information proprement dit (radio, télévision, etc.) est traité sous COMMUNICATIONS (DROIT DES).

PLATT, PRISCILLA, AND JEFFREY KAUFMAN	*Privacy Law in the Private Sector: An Annotation of the Legislation in Canada*	CLB (LL)
GRANOSIK, LUKASZ	Loi sur la protection des reseignements personnels dans le secteur privé, *Édition annotée, Législation – Jurisprudence*	Y Blais 2008
PERUN, HAYNA, MICHAEL ORR, AND FANNY DIMITRIADIS	*Guide to the Ontario Personal Health Information Protection Act*	Irwin 2005
DUPLESSIS, YVON	*L'accès à l'information et la protection des renseignements personnels : santé et services sociaux*	CCH 2005
DORAY, RAYMOND	Accès à l'information : *loi annotée, jurisprudence, analyse et commentaires*	Y Blais 2001
DRAPEAU, MICHAEL W., AND MARC-AURÈLE RACICOT	*Protection of Privacy in the Canadian Private Sector*	Crswl 2001
McNAIRN, COLIN H.H., AND ALEXANDER K. SCOTT	*Privacy Law in Canada*	LN/B 2001
QUÉBEC	*L'accès à l'information et la protection des renseignements personnels : loi indexée, commentée et annotée*	CCH 2001
McISAAC, BARBARA, RICK SHIELDS, AND KRIS KLEIN	*The Law of Privacy in Canada*	Crswl 2000
WOODBURY, CHRISTOPHER D., AND COLIN H.H. McNAIRN	*Government Information: Access & Privacy*	Crswl 1990

84.

PRIVATE INTERNATIONAL LAW

Private international law refers to legal disputes between private parties (whether individual persons or groups of individuals, such as associations or corporations) and either other private parties or the government of a state foreign to the private litigant. Often the litigation spends much of its time solving the conflict of laws question of which is the proper court to settle the dispute. Related topics: CONFLICT OF LAWS.

INTERNATIONAL PRIVÉ (DROIT)

Branche importante du droit civil, le nouveau *Code civil du Québec* lui consacre un livre entier (le dixième). La réputation de complexité du DIP en rebute plus d'un, mais la réalité transnationale et internationale moderne le rend inéluctable. Certains aspects commerciaux sont également abordés du point de vue du droit COMMERCIAL INTERNATIONAL.

WALKER, JANET	*Castel & Walker: Canadian Conflict of Laws*, 6th ed.	LN/B (LL)
EMANUELLI, CLAUDE	*Droit international privé québécois*, 2e éd.	W & LaF 2006
GUILLEMARD, SYLVETTE	*Le droit international privé face au contrat de vente cyberspatial*	Y Blais 2006
BACHAND, FRÉDÉRIC	*L'intervention du juge canadien avant et durant un arbitrage commercial international*	Y Blais 2005
BAER, MARVIN G., AND NICHOLAS RAFFERTY	*Private International Law in Common Law in Canada*, 2d ed.	EM 2003
CANADIAN BAR ASSOCIATION, CONTINUING LEGAL EDUCATION	*Public & Private International Law: What Every Lawyer Needs to Practice in Today's Global Community*	CBA 2000
FAWCETT, JAMES, AND PETER NORTH	*Cheshire and North's Private International Law*, 13th ed. (U.K.)	OUP 1999
CASTEL, J.-G.	*Private International Law: A Comparative Study of the Rules Prevailing in Canada and The United States*	CLB 1960

- PROCÉDURE CIVILE voir CIVIL PROCEDURE
- PROCÉDURE PÉNALE voir CRIMINAL PROCEDURE

PRODUCTS LIABILITY

This area of law is a particular subset within torts, and, more specifically, is usually regarded as a particular instance of negligence. Products liability cases most frequently arise when a defective product has in some way caused harm to the plaintiff. This is an area of provincial jurisdiction, but is guided primarily by principles established in the common law, many emanating from the famous English Court of Appeal decision, *Donoghue v. Stevenson* of the 1930s. Related topics: CLASS ACTIONS, NEGLIGENCE, SALE OF GOODS, TORTS.

RESPONSABILTÉ DU FAIT DES PRODUITS

Ce domaine relève à la fois de droit du CONSOMMATEUR et de la RESPONSABILITÉ CIVILE. Certaines lois statutaires apportent des précisions importantes.

THEALL, LAWRENCE G. *et al.*	*Product Liability: Canadian Law and Practice*	CLB (LL)
LINDEN, JUSTICE ALLEN, AND BRUCE FELDTHUSEN	"Products Liability," chapter 16 in *Canadian Tort Law*, 8th ed.	LN/B 2006
CASSELS, JAMIE	*The Law of Large-Scale Claims: Product Liability, Mass Torts, and Complex Litigation in Canada*	Irwin 2005
WADDAMS, STEPHEN M.	*Products Liability*, 4th ed.	Crswl 2002
EDGELL, DEAN F.	*Product Liability Law in Canada*	LN/B 2000

86.

PROFESSIONAL RESPONSIBILITY

Professional responsibility is usually associated with the self-regulated professions such as law, medicine, dentistry, and accountancy, the subject of professional responsibility deals with the ability of these professions to establish standards and rules of conduct and to impose sanctions upon members who breach these rules. These powers are delegated to the professions by way of provincial legislation. Related topics: CRIMINAL LAW, HEALTH LAW, LEGAL ETHICS, LEGAL PRACTICE, NEGLIGENCE, TORTS.

RESPONSABILITÉ PROFESSIONNELLE

Sous-ensemble de la RESPONSABILITÉ CIVILE. On étudie ici les règles particulières applicables aux divers professionnels régis par le *Code des professions*, les principes généraux demeurant les mêmes. Pour les autres aspects du droit applicable aux professionnels, voir : DISCIPLINAIRE (DROIT).

CASEY, JAMES T.	*The Regulation of Professions in Canada*	Crswl (LL)
MACKENZIE, GAVIN	*Lawyers & Ethics: Professional Responsibility and Discipline*	Crswl (LL)
ADAMSKI, JAKUB	"Legal Profession," a vol. of *Halsbury's Law of Canada*, 1st ed.	LN/B 2007
BEAUDOIN, JEAN-LOUIS ET PATRICE DESLAURIERS	*La responsabilité civile*, 7e éd. (2 vols.) *Principes généraux* (vol. 1) et *Responsabilité professionnelle* (vol. 2)	Y Blais 2007
VILLENEUVE, JEAN-GUY	*Précis de droit professionnel*	Y Blais 2007
HUTCHISON, ALLAN C.	*Legal Ethics and Professional Responsibility*, 2d ed.	Irwin 2006
GRAHAM, RANDAL	*Legal Ethics: Theories, Cases, and Professional Regulation*	EM 2004
GRANT, STEPHEN M., AND LINDA ROTHSTEIN	*Lawyers' Professional Liability*, 2d ed.	LN/B 1998
POIRIER, SYLVIE	*La discipline professionnelle au Québec : principes législatifs, jurisprudentiels et aspects pratiques*	Y Blais 1998
LAW SOCIETY OF MANITOBA	*Practice Before Professional Discipline Tribunals*	Law Society of Manitoba 1994

87.

PROPERTY

These titles deal with the law of property in general terms and leave the specifics of real property and intellectual property to separate listings. An important subtopic of this subject is bailment (the temporary placement of property with a second party). Property is an ancient area of the law that is firmly founded in the common law. Related topics: CONSTRUCTION LAW, CONTRACTS, FAMILY LAW, INTELLECTUAL PROPERTY LAW, PERSONAL PROPERTY SECURITY, REAL PROPERTY, TRUSTS.

BIENS ET PROPRIÉTÉ

Branche principale du droit civil. Le nouveau *Code civil* apporte quelques modifications et modernise l'ensemble. Le problème du droit des biens réside dans ses nombreux points de contact avec le droit public (aménagement et urbanisme, MUNICIPAL (DROIT), AGRICULTURE ET CULTURE HYDROPONIQUE, etc.). Certains aspects du droit des biens sont réglementés par des législations autonomes (par ex. VALEURS MOBILIÈRES).

BENSON, MARJORIE L.	*Understanding Property: A Guide to Canada's Property Law*	Crswl 2008
JOLI-COEUR, YVES ET OLIVIER J. BRANE	*Les copropriétés en difficulté : constats et solutions : France/Québec*	W & LaF 2007
JOLI-COEUR, YVES ET YVES PAPINEAU	*Code de la copropriété divise*	W & LaF 2007
LAFLAMME, LUCIE ET CHAMBRE DES NOTAIRES DU QUÉBEC	*La copropriété par indivision*, 2e éd.	Chambre des notaires du Québec 2007
LAFOND, PIERRE-CLAUDE	*Précis de droit des biens*, 2e éd.	Thémis 2007
FRENETTE, FRANÇOIS ET SYLVIO NORMAND	*Mélanges offerts au professeur François Frenette : études portant sur le droit patrimonial*	Université Laval 2006
ZIFF, BRUCE H.	*Principles of Property Law*, 4th ed.	Crswl 2006
LAMONTAGNE, DENYS CLAUDE	*Biens et propriété*, 5e éd.	Y Blais 2005
MOSSMAN, MARY JANE, AND WILLIAM F. FLANAGAN	*Property Law: Cases and Commentary*, 2d ed.	EM 2004
BASTARACHE, MICHEL	*Précis du droit des biens réels*, 2e éd.	Y Blais 2001
JAMES, ANDREW	"Bailment" in vol. 2, title 13 of the *Canadian Encyclopedic Digest* (Ontario) & (Western)	Crswl 1997
WELLING, BRUCE	*Property in Things in The Common Law System* (Aust.)	Scribblers 1996

88.

PUBLIC INTERNATIONAL LAW

Unlike private international law which deals with private persons and entities, public international law refers to the rules which govern nations in their dealings with other states. Treaties and international pacts are significant in this subject which is entirely federal in its jurisdiction. This subject also includes the law as it relates to armed conflict between nations. To understand this topic as it applies in Canada, it is not necessary to refer to exclusively Canadian sources. Related topics: INTERNATIONAL SALE OF GOODS, INTERNATIONAL TRADE LAW.

INTERNATIONAL PUBLIC (DROIT)

Branche du droit qui étudie les relations entre États souverains et certaines relations de particuliers avec un État étranger. Jadis cantonné aux questions de paix et de guerre, le droit international ne cesse de produire de nouvelles normes dans un grand nombre de domaines et influence ainsi le droit interne: ENVIRONNEMENT, TRAVAIL, TRANSPORTS (DROIT DES), PROPRIÉTÉ INTELLECTUELLE, MARITIME (DROIT), AÉRIEN (DROIT), pour ne mentionner que ces quelques exemples.

CURRIE, JOHN H.	*Public International Law*, 2d ed.	Irwin 2008
VAN ERT, GIBRAN	*Using International Law in Canadian Courts*, 2d ed.	Irwin 2008
CURRIE, JOHN H., CRAIG FORCESE, AND VALERIE OOSTERVELD	*International Law: Doctrine, Practice, and Theory*	Irwin 2007
BOTTING, GARY	*Canadian Extradition Law Practice*	LN/B 2005
GREEN, L.C.	*The Contemporary Law of Armed Conflict*, 2d ed.	Manchester University Press 1999
GREEN, L.C.	"International Law" in vol. 17, title 81 of the *Canadian Encyclopedic Digest* (Ontario)	Crswl 1995
EMANUELLI, CLAUDE	*Droit international public*, 2e éd.	W & LaF 1993
ARBOUR, JEAN-MAURICE	*Droit international public*, 2e éd.	Y Blais 1992

89.

REAL PROPERTY

This heading refers to property in the form of land, buildings, fixtures, etc. This is an area within the enunciated powers of the provinces by the *Constitution Act, 1867*. The principal concepts, however, are significantly informed by centuries of jurisprudence from England and the rest of the common-law world. Related topics: CONSTRUCTION LAW, LANDLORD & TENANT, MORTGAGES & LIENS, PROPERTY.

♦ Voir BIENS ET PROPRIÉTÉ sous PROPERTY

DI CASTRI, VICTOR	*The Law of Vendor and Purchaser*, 3d ed.	Crswl (LL)
LA FOREST, ANNE WARNER	*Anger & Honsberger Law of Real Property*, 3d ed.	CLB (LL)
LAMONT, DONALD H.L.	*Lamont on Real Estate Conveyancing*	Crswl (LL)
LAFOND, PIERRE-CLAUDE	*Précis de droit des biens*, 2e éd.	Thémis 2007
FRENETTE, FRANÇOIS ET SYLVIO NORMAND	*Mélanges offerts au professeur François Frenette : études portant sur le droit patrimonial*	Université Laval 2006
LAMONTAGNE, DENYS-CLAUDE	*Biens et propriété*, 5e éd.	Y Blais 2005
MCCALLUM, MARGARET, AND ALLAN M. SINCLAIR	*An Introduction to Real Property Law*, 5th ed.	LN/B 2005
BASTARACHE, MICHEL	*Précis du droit des biens réels*, 2e éd.	Y Blais 2001
PERELL, PAUL M., AND BRUCE H. ENGELL	*Remedies and the Sale of Land*, 2d ed.	LN/B 1998

♦ RECHERCHE DOCUMENTAIRE voir LEGAL RESEARCH
♦ RÉDACTION JURIDIQUE voir LEGAL WRITING

90.

REFUGEES

A subset of immigration and citizenship law, the law of refugees refers to the application for residency in Canada by persons from other countries who face persecution or danger were they to return to the countries from which they came. This is entirely within the federal sphere of activity and is governed by the federal *Immigration & Refugee Protection Act*. Related topic: IMMIGRATION & CITIZENSHIP.

RÉFUGIÉS

La question des réfugiés relève du droit INTERNATIONAL PUBLIC en raison surtout de l'existence de conventions internationales. Il importe de ne pas confondre avec le domaine plus vaste de l'IMMIGRATION. Le réfugié peut devenir immigrant, certes, mais l'immigrant n'est pas nécessairement un réfugié.

JONES, MARTIN, AND SASHA BAGLAY	*Refugee Law*	Irwin 2007
WALDMAN, LORNE	*Canadian Immigration & Refugee Law Practice 2008*	LN/B 2007
GALLOWAY, DAVID	"Canadian Refugee Law," Part Four in *Immigration Law*	Irwin 1997
BAGAMBIIRE, DAVIES B.N.	*Canadian Immigration and Refugee Law*	CLB 1996
MBUXI, BENJAMIN	*Les réfugiés et le droit international*	Crswl 1993
HATHAWAY, JAMES C.	*The Law of Refugee Status*	LN/B 1991
MATAS, DAVID	*Closing Doors: The Failure of Refugee Protection*	Summerhill Press 1989

◆ RÉGIMES DE RETRAITE voir PENSIONS

REMEDIES & RESTITUTION

The resolution of most legal disputes involves an order by the court for a particular remedy to be made to the aggrieved party. There is a range of remedies, from proscribing certain activities by one party (e.g., injunctions) to requiring compensation to the injured party (restitution). The primary basis for this area of law can be found in jurisprudence and also in court rules. Related topics: CIVIL PROCEDURE, CONTRACTS, DAMAGES, TORTS.

RESTITUTIONS DES PRESTATIONS

Nouveauté au *Code civil du Québec*, la restitution des prestations couvre uniformément un ensemble de situations où les parties reviennent à l'état antérieur à leurs engagements. C'est donc une conséquence de l'extinction des obligations. Voir aussi : CONTRATS ; OBLIGATIONS.

ROACH, KENT	*Constitutional Remedies*	CLB (LL)
BÉCHARD, DONALD	*Exécution des jugements*	Y Blais 2006
SMITH, LIONEL et al.	*The Law of Restitution in Canada: Cases, Notes, and Materials*	EM 2004
BERRYMAN, JEFFREY	*The Law of Equitable Remedies*	Irwin 2000
KLAR, LEWIS N.	*Remedies in Tort*	Crswl 2000
FRIDMAN, GERALD H. L.	*Restitution*, 2d ed.	Crswl 1992

- RESPONSABILITÉ CIVILE voir DAMAGES ; NEGLIGENCE ; NUISANCE ; OCCUPIER'S LIABILITY ; PRODUCTS LIABILITY ; TORTS
- RESSOURCES NATURELLES voir ENERGY & NATURAL RESOURCES LAW

92.

SALE OF GOODS

This topic deals with the sale of goods, which, roughly defined, means chattels and does not mean money, negotiable instruments, and land. Issues in this topic deal with the contractual nature of a sale, for example: defining formation or performance of the contract, terms of the sale (such as warranties and conditions), and transfer of title. This area of law is defined almost entirely by provincial statute, but informed by a wealth of jurisprudence. Related topics: CONSUMER PROTECTION LAW, CONTRACTS, INTERNATIONAL SALE OF GOODS.

VENTE

L'un des principaux contrats nommés prévus au *Code civil du Québec*, la vente fait l'objet de monographies particulières. On se rappellera que la VENTE INTERNATIONALE relève, quant à elle, d'une convention internationale spécifique, généralement étudiée avec le droit COMMERCIAL INTERNATIONAL.

BENJAMIN, J.P., ed.	*Benjamin's Sale of Goods*, 7th ed. (U.K.)	S & M 2008
ATIYAH, PATRICK S., JOHN N. ADAMS, AND HECTOR MACQUEEN	*The Sale of Goods*, 11th ed (U.K.)	Pearson Higher Education 2005
DESLAURIERS, JACQUES	*Vente, louage, contrat d'entreprise ou de service*	W & LaF 2005
LAMONTAGNE, DENYS-CLAUDE	*Droit de la vente*	Y Blais 2005
McGUINNESS, KEVIN PATRICK	*Sale and Supply of Goods*	LN/B 2005
FRIDMAN, GERALD H.L.	*Sales of Goods in Canada*, 5th ed.	Crswl 2004
LEVINSON, RICHARD E.	"Sale of Goods" in vol. 29, title 129 of the *Canadian Encyclopedic Digest* (Ontario)	Crswl 1998

- ◆ SANTÉ – MÉDECINE voir HEALTH LAW
- ◆ SANTÉ ET SÉCURITÉ AU TRAVAIL voir OCCUPATIONAL HEALTH & SAFETY
- ◆ SCOLAIRE (DROIT) voir EDUCATION LAW

93.

SECURITIES

This term has evolved over the centuries to its current common meaning, which is to refer to the shares and stocks of companies and corporations. The titles following in this listing relate primarily to the term "securities" in its reference to company shares and stocks. This is an area of primarily provincial jurisdiction with the provinces having securities acts. There is some federal interplay from some limited application of the *Bank Act*. Related topics: AGENCY, BANKING, COMMERCIAL LAW, CORPORATE LAW, TRUSTS.

VALEURS MOBILIÈRES

Domaine important et complexe du droit des AFFAIRES qui complète le droit des COMPAGNIES en traitant toute la question du contrôle public de l'émission des actions. Les valeurs mobilières sont de compétence provinciale malgré plusieurs tentatives d'interventions fédérales. L'Ontario assume le leadership canadien. On peut utiliser la jurisprudence américaine pour éclairer des notions particulières provenant de ce droit.

Borden Ladner Gervais (law firm)	*Securities Law and Practice*, 3d ed.	Crswl (LL)
Gagné, Suzanne	*Développements récents en valeurs mobilières*	Y Blais 2007
Gillen, Mark R.	*Securities Regulation in Canada*, 3d ed.	Crswl 2007
Proulx, Olivier	*Le traitement des porteurs minoritaires dans un contexte transactionnel*	W & LaF 2007
Johnston, David, and Kathleen Rockwell	*Canadian Securities Regulation*, 4th ed.	LN/B 2006
Condon, M.G., Anita Anand, and Janis P. Sarra	*Securities Law in Canada: Cases and Commentary*	EM 2005
Turcotte, Carole	*Le droit des valeurs mobilières*	Y Blais 2005
Petraglia, Philip, and Lazar Sarna	*Corporate Securities Law in Canada*	Condor Books 2003
MacIntosh, Jeffrey G., and Christopher Nichols	*Securities Law*	Irwin 2002

94.

SENTENCING

According to the federal *Criminal Code,* sentences are imposed upon those convicted of criminal infractions with the intention of expressing society's denunciation of the crime, deterring the transgressor from further similar activity, promoting in the offenders a sense of responsibility for their malfeasance, and assisting in the offender's rehabilitation. There is a significant body of law, entirely federal and predominantly statutory, which directs judges in the formulation of sentences. Related topics: CRIMINAL LAW, CRIMINAL PROCEDURE, HUMAN RIGHTS AND THE *CHARTER OF RIGHTS AND FREEDOMS,* YOUNG OFFENDERS.

SENTENCES

Les sentences sont des décisions punitives prises par les tribunaux en DROIT CRIMINEL ou en droit pénal. Certaines dimensions relèvent de la PROCÉDURE PÉNALE. Les conditions d'exécution de ces sentences peuvent relever du droit CARCÉRAL.

RUBY, CLAYTON C. *et al.*	*Sentencing,* 6th ed.	LN/B 2008
DADOUR, FRANÇOIS	*De la détermination de la peine : principes et applications*	LexisNexis 2007
FERRIS, JUDGE T.W.	*Sentencing: Practical Approaches*	LN/B 2005
RENAUD, GILLES	*Principes de la détermination de la peine*	Y Blais 2004
PICKARD, TONI, PHILIP GOLDMAN, AND ROSE-MARY CAIRNS-WAY	"Sentencing: Rules and Dilemmas," chapter 2 in *Dimensions of Criminal Law,* 3d ed.	EM 2002
MANSON, ALLAN	*The Law of Sentencing*	Irwin 2001
DUMONT, HÉLÈNE	*Pénologie : le droit canadien relatif aux peines et aux sentences*	Thémis 1993
COLE, DAVID, AND ALLAN MANSON	*Release from Imprisonment: The Law of Sentencing, Parole, and Judicial Review*	Crswl 1990
NADIN-DAVID, R. PAUL	*Sentencing in Canada*	Crswl 1982

* SOCIÉTÉS ET ASSOCIATIONS voir PARTNERSHIPS

95.

STATUTES & STATUTORY INTERPRETATION

This listing deals with the process of enacting statutes and statutory instruments and the various approaches used in their interpretation. Related topics: LEGAL REASONING, LEGAL RESEARCH, LEGAL WRITING.

INTERPRÉTATION DES LOIS

Méthodologie fondamentale du droit, les principes et mécanismes de l'interprétation couvrent universellement les domaines et les types de lois. Le fond du droit statutaire provenant du droit anglais, c'est de ce côté qu'on se tournera pour compléter les sources québécoises et canadiennes, sauf en droit civil où les règles d'interprétation empruntent à une autre logique.

SULLIVAN, RUTH	*Statutory Interpretation*, 2d ed.	Irwin 2007
SULLIVAN, RUTH	*Sullivan and Driedger on the Construction of Statutes*, 4th ed.	LN/B 2002
GRAHAM, RANDY N.	*Statutory Interpretation: Theory and Practice*	EM 2001
COTÉ, PIERRE-ANDRÉ	*The Interpretation of Legislation in Canada*, 3d ed.	Crswl 2000
CÔTÉ, PIERRE-ANDRÉ	*Interprétation des lois*	Thémis 1999
GIFFORD, DONALD J.	*How to Understand Statutes and By-Laws*	Crswl 1996
PIGEON, LOUIS-PHILLIPE	*Drafting and Interpreting Legislation*	Crswl 1988

♦ SUCCESSIONS voir WILLS & ESTATES

96.

TAXATION

This listing deals with taxation in general and some specific types of taxation (excluding income tax). By virtue of the *Constitution Act, 1867*, the federal government can raise taxes directly or indirectly, whereas the provinces may only raise taxes directly. Taxes dealt with under this topic include sales taxes (both federal and provincial), corporate taxes, resource taxation, property taxes, *inter alia*. This a multi-jurisdictional area (federal, provincial, and municipal). There is an international context as well, via the various bilateral tax treaties to which Canada is signatory. Related topics: AGRICULTURAL & AQUACULTURE LAW, INTERNATIONAL TRADE LAW, MUNICIPAL LAW, PUBLIC INTERNATIONAL LAW, REAL PROPERTY, TAXATION (INCOME TAX).

FISCALITÉ

Domaine important du droit public où le fédéral et le Québec exercent compétences et activités. L'abondance des publications ne risque pas de dissiper la complexité du domaine qui en rebute plus d'un. Là triomphent le cas particulier et la disposition transitoire, la multiplicité et l'enchevêtrement des textes.

HANSON, SUZANNE I.R.	*Canada Tax Manual*	Crswl (LL)
HULL, BARRY R.	*GST & Commodity Tax*	Crswl (LL)
KRISHNA, VERN	*Canada's Tax Treaties*	LN/B (LL)
SHERMAN, DAVID M.	*Basic Tax and GST Guide for Lawyers 2006–07*	Crswl 2006
TOBIAS, NORMAN C.	*Taxation of Corporations, Partnerships, and Trusts*, 3d ed.	Crswl 2006
LORD, GUY	*Les principes de l'imposition au Canada*	W & LaF 2002
CANADA ET QUÉBEC	*La loi du praticien TPS-TVQ annotée*	Crswl 1997

97.

TAXATION (INCOME TAX)

Income tax is both a federal matter (the *Income Tax Act*) and a provincial one (there is an income tax act in each of the provinces). There is an enormous amount of taxation litigation and research undertaken every day in Canada and a wealth of resources available to interested parties. Sources dealing with corporate income tax are listed under taxation. This listing deals with works that are focused on the taxation of personal income. Related topics: TAXATION, TRUSTS.

FISCALITÉ (IMPÔT SUR LE REVENU)

Domaine important du droit public où le fédéral et le Québec exercent compétences et activités. L'abondance des publications ne risque pas de dissiper la complexité du domaine qui en rebute plus d'un. Là triomphent le cas particulier et la disposition transitoire, la multiplicité et l'enchevêtrement des textes.

Tari, A. Christina	*Federal Income Tax Litigation in Canada*	LN/B (LL)
Duff, David G. *et al.*	*Canadian Income Tax Law*, 2d ed.	LN/B 2006
Duff, David G.	*Canadian Income Tax Law: Cases, Texts, and Materials*	EM 2002
Lord, Guy	*Les principes de l'imposition au Canada*	W & LaF 2002
Gorman, Barry	*Canadian Income Taxation: Policy and Practice*, 2d ed.	Crswl 2001
Krishna, Vern	*Income Tax Law*	Irwin 1997

• TECHNOLOGIES DE L'INFORMATION (DROIT DES) voir INFORMATION TECHNOLOGY LAW

98.

TORTS

The general term applied to civil wrongs which give rise to a cause of action by one party against another. A number of specific torts have been dealt with individually in this book. This listing looks at general works dealing with the broad concepts surrounding this subject such as strict liability, remoteness, intentional torts, *inter alia*. Related topics: CLASS ACTIONS, DAMAGES, DEFAMATION, HEALTH LAW, NEGLIGENCE, NUISANCE, OCCUPIER'S LIABILITY, PRIVACY LAW & ACCESS TO INFORMATION, PRODUCTS LIABILITY, REMEDIES & RESTITUTION, WRONGFUL DISMISSAL.

RESPONSABILITÉ CIVILE

Branche majeure du droit civil et partie importante du domaine des OBLIGATIONS.

KLAR, LEWIS N.	*Tort Law*, 4th ed.	Crswl 2008
BAUDOUIN, JEAN-LOUIS	*La responsabilité civile*	Y Blais 2007
OSBORNE, PHILIP H.	*The Law of Torts*, 3d ed.	Irwin 2007
BARREAU DU QUÉBEC	*Les dommages en matière civile et commerciale*	Y Blais 2006
LINDEN, JUSTICE ALLEN, AND BRUCE FELDTHUSEN	*Canadian Tort Law*, 8th ed.	LN/B 2006
WEINRIB, ERNEST	*Tort Law: Cases and Materials*, 2d ed.	EM 2003
FRIDMAN, GERALD H. L.	*The Law of Torts in Canada*, 2d ed.	Crswl 2002

99.

TRADE-MARKS

A subset of intellectual property, trade marks are symbols or sayings associated with a particular brand or service and are protected by the federal *Trade-marks Act* and the registration of trade-marks with the Register of Trade-marks. There has been a substantial increase in research activity in this topic with the advent of the internet and the possibilities it presents for the infringement of copyright, and other issues related to domain names (such as cyber-squatting). This is an entirely federal area of activity, but there is a substantial body of caselaw associated with the subject. Related topics: INTELLECTUAL PROPERTY LAW.

MARQUES DE COMMERCE

Sous-ensemble de la propriété intellectuelle, le droit des marques de commerce couvre spécifiquement les noms des produits et des entreprises qu'on veut protéger par la loi. Le droit des AFFAIRES s'intéresse à ces notions analogues au droit d'AUTEUR.

BURSHTEIN, SHELDON	*Domain Names and Internet Trade-mark Issues: Canadian Law and Practice*	Crswl (LL)
HUGHES, HON. ROGER T., TONI ASHTON, AND NEAL ARMSTRONG	*Hughes on Trade Marks*, 2d ed.	LN/B (LL)
RICHARD, HUGUES G., AND LAURENT CARRIÈRE	*Robic Leger Annotated* Trade-marks Act	Crswl (LL)
HUGHES, HON. ROGER T., AND TONI POLSON ASHTON	"Trade-Marks, Passing Off and Unfair Competition," a vol. of *Halsbury's Laws of Canada*, 1st ed.	LN/B 2007
HUGHES, JUSTICE ROGER T.	Trade-marks Act *& Commentary*, 2006–07 ed.	LN/B 2006
CANADA	*Loi canadienne sur les marques de commerce annotée*	Crswl 2000
VAVER, DAVID	"Trade-Marks," chapter 4 in *Intellectual Property Law: Copyright, Patents, and Trade-Marks*	Irwin 1997

TRANSPORTATION LAW

This topic deals with the law as it relates to various modes of transportation (excluding aviation law, maritime law, and motor vehicle law, which are dealt with separately). Topics include carriage of goods and passengers, railways, and trucking, etc. As most transportation in Canada is interprovincial, this is an area of primarily federal jurisdiction, governed by various federal statutes, (e.g., the *Canada Transportation Act*, the *Department of Transport Act*, the *Aeronautics Act*, and the *Railway Safety Act*). There are, however, some provincial statutes governing transportation exclusively within their borders. A number of provinces have railway acts and most have legislation dealing with the transportation of hazardous goods (as does the federal government by virtue of the *Hazardous Products Act*). Related topics: AVIATION & AERONAUTICS LAW, MOTOR VEHICLE LAW.

TRANSPORTS (DROIT DES)

Domaine très réglementé autant que peu documenté. À part le fait que le contrat de transport est un des contrats nommés, la complexité du droit des transports tient à la fois du droit CONSTITUTIONNEL (par ex., transport local vs interprovincial et international, ce dernier étant régi par les conventions) et aux divers moyens de transport (par ex., aérien, maritime, terrestre). Outre la réglementation étatique applicable, il faut tenir compte de l'apport des parties au contrat, et ce, particulièrement en droit COMMERCIAL INTERNATIONAL.

JOLIN, LOUIS	*Droit du tourisme au Québec*	Presse de l'Université du Québec 2005
MCNEIL, JOHN S.	*Motor Carrier Cargo Claims*, 5th ed.	Crswl 2007
FERNANDES, RUI	*Transportation Law*	Crswl 1991–2000
PORTMAN, ELIZABETH	"Railways" in vol. 28, title 122 of the *Canadian Encyclopedic Digest* (Ontario) and vol. 29, title 124 of the *Canadian Encyclopedic Digest* (Western)	Crswl 1997
SOJAK, JOHN P.	"Carriers" in vol. 4, title 23 of the *Canadian Encyclopedic Digest* (Ontario) and vol. 5, title 23 of the *Canadian Encyclopedic Digest* (Western)	Crswl 1995

- TRAVAIL voir EMPLOYMENT LAW; LABOUR LAW

TRUSTS

The law of trusts is a very old and complicated area of property law that originated centuries ago in England. At its core is the notion that property can be held by one party (the trustee) for the benefit of another person, either the party entrusting the property to the trustee (known as the beneficiary) or even for a third party. The trustee must always deal with the property in the best interests of the beneficiary. Trusts can be express or implied (i.e., inferred by a court). Related topics: AGENCY, CHARITIES & CHARITABLE CORPORATIONS, CONTRACTS, FAMILY LAW, PROPERTY, REAL PROPERTY, TAXATION, WILLS & ESTATES.

FIDUCIE

Grand apport scientifique de la common law au droit romain, le trust de droit anglais entre de plein droit dans le nouveau *Code civil*, non sans quelques ajustements. L'institution à sa place à côté des mécanismes d'administration des biens d'autrui et complète le pan du droit relatif aux BIENS ET PROPRIÉTÉ.

GILLEN, MARK, AND FAYE WOODMAN	*The Law of Trusts: A Contextual Approach*, 2d ed.	EM 2008
BECKER, RAINER	*Die fiducie von Quebec und der trust: ein Vergleich mit verscheidenen Modellen fiduziarischer Rechtsfiguren im civil law*	Mohr Siebeck 2007
CARON, PATRICK-CLAUDE	*Guide pratique sur les successions et fiducies*	CCH 2007
BEAULNE, JACQUES	*Droit des fiducies*	W & LaF 2005
GILLESE, JUSTICE EILEEN E., AND MARTHA MILCZYNSKI	*The Law of Trusts*, 2d ed.	Irwin 2005
WATERS, DONOVAN W.M., MARK GILLEN, AND LIONEL SMITH	*Waters' Law of Trusts in Canada*, 3d ed.	Crswl 2005
OOSTERHOFF, A.H. *et al.*	*Oosterhoff on Trusts: Text, Commentary, and Materials*, 6th ed.	Crswl 2004
CANTIN CUMYN, MADELEINE	*L'administration du bien d'autrui*	Y Blais 2000
YOUDAN, TIMOTHY G.	*Equity, Fiduciaries, and Trusts*	Crswl 1989

+ VALEURS MOBILIÈRES voir SECURITIES
+ VENTE voir SALE OF GOODS
+ VENTE INTERNATIONALE voir INTERNATIONAL SALE OF GOODS

102.

WILLS & ESTATES

Family estate planning involves a number of different legal devices for the transferral of property after one's death. A will is the most commonly employed, but trusts are also frequently used. As this topic deals with property, it is fully in the sphere of the provinces' articulated powers and each has legislative acts dealing with the administration of estates. Related topics: FAMILY LAW, PROPERTY, TRUSTS.

SUCCESSIONS

Branche du droit civil, les successions occupent un livre entier du *Code civil du Québec*. La planification successorale est souvent étudiée avec la FISCALITÉ.

MacKenzie, James	*Feeney's Canadian Law of Wills*, 4th ed.	LN/B (LL)
Caron, Patrick-Claude	*Guide pratique sur les successions et fiducies*	CCH 2007
Le May, Sylvie et Mariève Lacroix	*La liquidation et le partage de la succession : (Art. 776 à 898 C.c.Q.) : extraits du Droit civil en ligne*	Y Blais 2007
Harvey, Cameron, and Linda Vincent	*The Law of Dependant's Relief in Canada*, 2d ed.	Crswl 2006
Fazakas, Derek	*Wills and Estates*, 2d ed.	EM 2004
MacGregor, Mary L.	*Preparation of Wills and Power of Attorney: First Interview to Final Report*, 3d ed.	CLB 2004
Brière, Germain	*Droit des successions*	W & LaF 2002
Allen, William, and John Pearson Allen	*Estate Planning Handbook*, 3d ed.	Crswl 1999

WORKERS' COMPENSATION

Workers' compensation schemes are in operation in every province in order to compensate injured workers without the necessity of entering into civil litigation to sue for recompense. Not only would litigation be difficult for many workers, the common law would often fail to recognize a head under which claimants could sue. This is an area of provincial jurisdiction and there are workers' compensation acts in all provinces (slightly different titles are used in Newfoundland and Labrador and Ontario). Related topics: EMPLOYMENT LAW, INSURANCE LAW, LABOUR LAW, OCCUPATIONAL HEALTH & SAFETY, TORTS.

ACCIDENTS DU TRAVAIL ET MALADIES PROFESSIONELLES

Ce domaine relève globalement de la sécurité sociale. Il touche le cas particulier des accidents survenus sur les lieux ou à cause du travail. Les grands traités du TRAVAIL abordent ces questions.

BRADET, DENIS	*La Loi sur les accidents du travail et les maladies professionnelles : aspects pratiques et juridiques*, 6e éd.	Y Blais 2007
ONTARIO BAR ASSOCIATION	*Advanced Workers' Compensation: New Directions and Best Practices in Return to Work*	Ontario Bar Association 2005
DEE, GARTH, AND NICK McCOMBIE	*Workers' Compensation in Ontario Handbook*, rev. ed.	LN/B 1999
ROBIN, JULIET S.	"Workers' Compensation" in vol. 34, title 151 of the *Canadian Encyclopedic Digest* (Ontario)	Crswl 1998
ISON, TERENCE G.	*Compensation Systems for Injury and Disease: The Policy Choices*	LN/B 1994
ISON, TERENCE G.	*Workers' Compensation in Canada*, 2d ed.	LN/B 1989

WRONGFUL DISMISSAL

Wrongful dismissal refers to the improper termination of employment either through outright dismissal (e.g., firing) or through constructive dismissal (significantly altering an employee's job as to effectively redefine it). Like employment law, this is an area of provincial jurisdiction and is guided mostly by principles established in caselaw. Related topics: EMPLOYMENT LAW, LABOUR LAW, TORTS.

CONGÉDIEMENT

Aspect particulier du droit du TRAVAIL. C'est dans le contexte particulier du contrat individuel de travail que le problème se pose; rappelons que ce contrat est l'un des contrats nommés prévus au *Code civil du Québec*.

LEVITT, HOWARD A.	*The Law of Dismissal in Canada*, 3d ed.	CLB (LL)
MOLE, ELLEN E., AND MARION J. STENDON	*Wrongful Dismissal Practice Manual*, 2d ed.	LN/B (LL)
HARRIS, DAVID	*Wrongful Dismissal*	Crswl (LL)
ENGLAND, GEOFFREY	*Individual Employment Law*, 2d ed.	Irwin 2008
CORRY, DAVID, AND SHARON CARTMILL	"Wrongful Dismissal" in vol. 35, title 153 of the *Canadian Encyclopedic Digest* (Western)	Crswl 2000
CORRY, DAVID J., AND JAMES M. PETRIE	*Conducting a Wrongful Dismissal Action, 1996*	Crswl 1997
LAPORTE, PIERRE	*Le traité du recours à l'encontre du congédiement sans cause juste et suffisante*	W & LaF 1992
AUDET, GEORGES et al.	*Le congédiement en droit québécois en matière de contrat individuel de travail*, 3e éd.	Y Blais 1991

105.

YOUNG OFFENDERS

The primary purpose of having a separate criminal law for persons under a certain age is to protect them from entry into the adult criminal justice system in the belief that there is a far greater likelihood of eventual rehabilitation should they remain outside that system. This is an area of federal jurisdiction (as is the criminal law generally) and is governed largely by the *Youth Criminal Justice Act* (which was formerly the *Young Offenders Act* and, even earlier, the *Juvenile Delinquents Act*). Provisions of the federal *Criminal Code* and *Canada Evidence Act* are also at play in this area of law. Related topics: CHILDREN AND THE LAW, CRIMINAL LAW, CRIMINAL PROCEDURE, EVIDENCE (CRIMINAL).

JEUNES CONTREVENANTS

Cette expression vise spécifiquement le sous-ensemble du droit pénal et du droit CRIMINEL qui s'applique à la JEUNESSE.

HARRIS, JUSTICE PETER	Youth Criminal Justice Act *Manual*	CLB (LL)
OLIVO, LAURENCE, RALPH COTTER, AND REBECCA BROMWICH	*Youth and the Law: New Approaches to Criminal Justice and Child Protection*	EM 2006
TUSTIN, LEE, AND ROBERT E. LUTES	*A Guide to the* Youth Criminal Justice Act, *2007*	LN/B 2006
BRYANT, MARIAN E.	"Young Offenders" in vol. 34, title 152 of the *Canadian Encyclopedic Digest* (Ontario) and in Volume 35, title 154 of the *Canadian Encyclopedic Digest* (Western)	Crswl 2004
MERCIER, CARL	*Loi sur le système de justice pénale pour les adolescents & Loi sur la protection de la jeunesse : recueil annoté*	Éditions juridiques FD 2004
BALA, NICHOLAS	*Youth Criminal Justice Law*	Irwin 2002
PLATT, PRISCILLA	*Young Offenders Law in Canada,* 2d ed.	LN/B 1995

About the Authors

John Eaton, LL.B. (Toronto), M.L.S. (Maryland) is the Law Librarian and Associate Professor of Law at the University of Manitoba where he teaches advanced legal research. He is past president of Canadian Association of Law Libraries/Association Canadienne des bibliotheques de droit.

Denis Le May is the former law librarian at Université Laval, and the author of many books and articles. He has written a definitive French treatise on legal research, as well as the chapter on Québec research in Douglass T. MacEllven's *Legal Research Handbook*. He is the author of *The Civil Code of Québec in Chart Form* which was published by Irwin Law in 2006 and which is based on his *Le code civil du Québec en tableaux synoptiques* (Wilson & Lafleur, 1992). He is past president of Canadian Association of Law Libraries/Association Canadienne des bibliotheques de droit.